BY HEART

BY HEART
101 Poems to Remember

Edited
with an introduction by
TED HUGHES

faber and faber

First published in 1997
by Faber and Faber Limited
3 Queen Square London WC1N 3AU

Photoset by Wilmaset Ltd, Wirral
Printed in England by Clays Ltd, St Ives plc

A CIP record for this book
is available from the British Library

ISBN 0−571−19263−7

6 8 10 9 7 5

Contents

Memorising Poems

There are many reasons for learning poems. But memorising them should be like a game. It should be a pleasure.

For those of us who need help (nearly all of us), the method most commonly used in schools is *learning by rote*. This is only one of several memorising techniques. And for most people it is the least effective. The tedium of learning by rote was long thought to be a good thing in English classrooms: disciplinary and character-building. But the cost can be heavy, since it creates an aversion to learning and to poetry.

Those who dislike rote-learning yet still wish to gain the many powers that come with knowledge can choose from an array of other less laborious, more productive, more amusing techniques.

These techniques systematically exploit the brain's natural tactics for remembering. Recently I heard one sound technician in a theatre questioning the other about the letters GBH, which kept appearing in some music-schedule for a play. It was explained: GBH was one of the actors. But instead of trying to remember the actor's name, the technician had simply dubbed him Ginger Beer Hair. This is the sort of thing we all do almost without thinking about it.

But why should the actor's name be so forgettable while the idea of his head being a foaming mass of Ginger Beer Hair is instantly and without effort unforgettable – and amusing into the bargain?

One of the brain's spontaneous techniques for fixing anything in the conscious memory, in other words for making it easy to recall, is to connect it with a visual image. And the more absurd, exaggerated, grotesque that image is, the more unforgettable is the thing to which we connect it. One easy technique for memorising poems uses visualised images in this way.

Basically, this particular technique is good for memorising lists. For example:

A peaty burn (stream)
A brown horse
An avalanche
A roaring lion
A hen-coop
A comb
A fleece
Foam
A flute
A lake
Home

might be dealt with as follows:

For 'peaty burn' it might be enough simply to imagine, like a frame in a colour film, a dark torrential mountain stream coming down among boulders. But to make sure it is 'burn' and not 'stream' that you remember, it might be better to imagine the stream actually burning, sending up flames and smoke: a cascade of dark fire, scorching the banks.

The next item, 'brown horse', now has to be connected to the burning stream. The most obvious short-cut is to put the horse in the torrent of fire, trying to scramble out – possibly with its mane in flames.

The next item, 'avalanche', now has to be connected to the brown horse. Imagine the burnt horse fleeing across the hillside from the burning stream, creating an avalanche, and galloping among the big, rolling rocks, its mane smoking.

The next item, 'a roaring lion', has to be connected to the avalanche. The boulders could be imagined pouring down onto the head of a huge, sleepy lion, who wakes up shaking them from his mane and roaring.

The next item, 'a hen-coop', has to be connected to that lion. Imagine the lion fleeing from the boulders to hide in – of all places – a hen-coop. He squeezes himself inside, grabbing and swallowing the hens to make more room.

The next item, 'a comb', has to be connected to the coop. The lion has burst from the coop and gone. So now you construct a rickety, awkward, great comb out of the splintered slats of the hen-coop – try combing your own hair with it.

And so on. If each image is 'photographed' mentally, as on a screen, it will not be forgotten easily. And each image will bring on the next which has been connected to it. Even when you are remembering a very long list, the procedure is quite small-scale and automatic because you are never remembering more than one connection at a time and each connection provides you with the next. The rolling rocks produce – surprise – the lion. The lion produces – out of nowhere and against all expectations – the hen-coop. The hen-coop produces – can it be right? – the ridiculous wooden comb.

Theoretically, if each connecting image is visualised successfully, the list can be endless, because each step will always produce the next.

The same technique is used by professional memorisers for memorising poems. Some readers may have recognised the list above. The first four lines of Hopkins's poem

'Inversnaid' go:

> This darksome burn, horseback brown,
> His rollrock highroad roaring down,
> In coop and in comb the fleece of his foam
> Flutes and low to the lake falls home.

Using the simple technique described, the lines can be memorised phrase by phrase by converting the poem to a kind of list. The same list as above, but now based on the words of the poem:

> Darksome burn
> Horseback brown
> Rollrock highroad
> Roaring down
> Coop
> Comb
> Fleece
> Foam
> Flutes
> Lake
> Home

In each case the visual image will be enough to do two things: to bring back the verbal phrase in which it is now rooted and to bring on the next image. Once visually fixed, whenever the sequence is started with the image of the mountain torrent of dark fire the whole film will replay itself and the words of the poem will come with it as the soundtrack.

Hopkins's poem is made up of solid objects. With poems composed in more abstract language the memoriser has to use more ingenuity – but since anything is permitted a way can always be found.

Some may meet a difficulty in releasing the imagination enough to produce the visual images for the cartoon. But practice helps. The release of playful imagination also releases energy, and the brain soon becomes skilful at what it enjoys.

Others may feel reluctant to add such an arbitrary cartoon accompaniment to the sacred words of a solemn poem. But the cartoon is only a first stage. The whole point is to get the poem, by any means, foul or fair, into the head. After a few replays, the words enter the long-term memory, and the cartoon begins to fall away.

In this description I have assumed that the memoriser's mental film of unforgettable images will always supply the perfect wording of each phrase. How does this happen, if each unforgettable image is anchored, as a rule, to no more than one key word in the phrase to which it corresponds? Is that one key word really enough to trigger the memory of all the other words in the phrase? In practice, for most people, where the text being learned is a poem worth learning, the answer is yes. Conscious use of visual imagination brings us to the key-word – but at that point another kind of imagination takes over. Without conscious effort, what then comes to our help is musical or audial memory. In many people, the audial memory is much stronger than the visual. It is wide open to any distinct pattern of sounds. It likes such patterns, and has an extraordinary ability to hang on to them whether we want them or not – as with musical melodies.

The closest thing to a musical melody in a line of verse is the pattern of sounds made by the sequence of syllables. That pattern includes rhythm and overall inflection along with the alternation of vowels and consonants. The stronger the pattern is, the more memorable the line will be. I remember back in 1959 Heinz advertised a competition for a catch-phrase to advertise their beans. Following the precedent of old oral poetry, using alliteration, assonance and internal rhyme, I came up with 'Whoever minds how he dines demands Heinz.' I realised this was cumbersome, but I still couldn't get it out of my head, so I took it no further, and sent it in. What they ended up with, of course, was the inspired 'Beanz meanz Heinz' – using exactly the same principle as I had, but in that simpler, more concentrated pattern. Even nonsense becomes memorable if the sound pattern is strong enough. The line in Wilfred Owen's poem 'Strange Meeting'

None will break ranks though nations trek from progress

is not exactly meaningless, but is so rhetorically overblown that only two things justify its place in the poem: it sounds magnificent and it is unforgettable. The interplay of 'breakra-', 'trekfro-' and 'progress' is glaringly contrived but, as in the old Welsh poetry from which Owen drew the system, it does what it is meant to do – it roots itself directly in the nerves of the ear.

These examples rely on a dominant pattern in the interwoven textures of the syllables. But a line can be just as unforgettable where the dominant pattern is one of rhythm, as in 'Tom, Tom, the piper's son.' Or where it is one of inflection, as in 'Och, Johnny, I hardly knew ye!', which Yeats called the most passionate phrase in the language.

Where lines of verse are less strikingly patterned, it may be that the audial imagination grasps them less tenaciously, less automatically. But in most verse worth remembering, the lines always yield some kind of pattern, though often the pattern is hidden, and not so much 'heard' as 'sensed through hearing'. In our own language verbal sounds are organically linked to the vast system of root-meanings and related associations, deep in the subsoil of psychological life, beyond our immediate awareness or conscious manipulation. It is the distinction of poetry to create strong patterns in these hidden meanings as well as in the clearly audible sounds. The hidden patterns are, if anything, much the stronger. The audial memory picks up those patterns in the depths from what it hears at the surface. And they too are difficult to forget. We feel them almost as a physical momentum of inevitability, a current of syntactical force purposefully directed like the flight of an arrow in the dark. What is essential, then, in memorising verse, is to keep the audial faculty wide open, and not so much look at the words as listen for them – listening as widely, deeply and keenly as possible, testing every whisper on the air in the echo-chamber of your whole body, as you bend more narrowly over the job of making that film of brightly coloured images.

Memory techniques of the kind I have described, using strongly visualised imagery, were invented in the ancient world and became the basis of learning in the Christian Middle Ages, when books were scarce. They were taken for granted, regarded as essential, and developed further by such giants of learning as St Thomas Aquinas, the angelic Doctor of the Catholic Church who has been called the patron saint of memory systems, and who made the unforgettable remark: 'Man cannot understand without images.'

In England in the seventeenth century, the Puritan/Protestant ascendancy of the Civil War made a serious bid to eradicate imagery from all aspects of life – methodically destroying the religious imagery of churches and forbidding the imaginative play of drama. The same spirit also banished from the schools the old-established memory techniques that used 'imagery' and officially replaced them with 'learning by rote'. The discarded methods, dimly associated with Paganism and Catholicism, were soon forgotten. If any attempt was made to reintroduce them, they were dismissed as 'tricks' and 'cheating'. 'Learning by rote' became the norm.

BY HEART

'Thrice the brinded cat hath mew'd'

Thrice the brinded cat hath mew'd.
Thrice and once the hedge-pig whin'd.
Harper cries: 'Tis time, 'tis time.
Round about the cauldron go;
In the poison'd entrails throw.
Toad, that under cold stone
Days and nights hast thirty-one
Swelter'd venom sleeping got,
Boil thou first i' the charmed pot.
   Double, double toil and trouble;
   Fire burn and cauldron bubble.

Fillet of a fenny snake,
In the cauldron boil and bake;
Eye of newt, and toe of frog,
Wool of bat, and tongue of dog,
Adder's fork, and blind-worm's sting,
Lizard's leg, and howlet's wing,
For a charm of powerful trouble,
Like a hell-broth boil and bubble.
   Double, double toil and trouble;
   Fire burn and cauldron bubble.

Scale of dragon, tooth of wolf,
Witches' mummy, maw and gulf
Of the ravin'd salt-sea shark,
Root of hemlock digg'd i' the dark,
Liver of blaspheming Jew,
Gall of goat, and slips of yew
Sliver'd in the moon's eclipse,

Nose of Turk, and Tartar's lips,
Finger of birth-strangled babe
Ditch-deliver'd by a drab,
Make the gruel thick and slab:
Add thereto a tiger's chaudron,
For the ingredients of our cauldron.
    Double, double toil and trouble;
    Fire burn and cauldron bubble.
    Cool it with a baboon's blood,
    Then the charm is firm and good.

ALFRED, LORD TENNYSON

The Eagle

He clasps the crag with crooked hands;
Close to the sun in lonely lands,
Ring'd with the azure world, he stands.

The wrinkled sea beneath him crawls;
He watches from his mountain walls,
And like a thunderbolt he falls.

from A Shropshire Lad

On Wenlock Edge the wood's in trouble;
    His forest fleece the Wrekin heaves;
The gale, it plies the saplings double,
    And thick on Severn snow the leaves.

'Twould blow like this through holt and hanger
    When Uricon the city stood:
'Tis the old wind in the old anger,
    But then it threshed another wood.

Then, 'twas before my time, the Roman
    At yonder heaving hill would stare:
The blood that warms an English yeoman,
    The thoughts that hurt him, they were there.

There, like the wind through woods in riot,
    Through him the gale of life blew high;
The tree of man was never quiet:
    Then 'twas the Roman, now 'tis I.

The gale, it plies the saplings double,
    It blows so hard, 'twill soon be gone:
To-day the Roman and his trouble
    Are ashes under Uricon.

James I

The child of Mary Queen of Scots,
　　A shifty mother's shiftless son,
Bred up among intrigues and plots,
　　Learnèd in all things, wise in none.
Ungainly, babbling, wasteful, weak,
　　Shrewd, clever, cowardly, pedantic,
The sight of steel would blanch his cheek.
　　The smell of baccy drive him frantic.
He was the author of his line –
　　He wrote that witches should be burnt;
He wrote that monarchs were divine,
　　And left a son who – proved they weren't!

The Road Not Taken

Two roads diverged in a yellow wood,
And sorry I could not travel both
And be one traveler, long I stood
And looked down one as far as I could
To where it bent in the undergrowth;

Then took the other, as just as fair,
And having perhaps the better claim,
Because it was grassy and wanted wear;
Though as for that, the passing there
Had worn them really about the same,

And both that morning equally lay
In leaves no step had trodden black.
Oh, I kept the first for another day!
Yet knowing how way leads on to way,
I doubted if I should ever come back.

I shall be telling this with a sigh
Somewhere ages and ages hence:
Two roads diverged in a wood, and I –
I took the one less traveled by,
And that has made all the difference.

The Fall of Rome

for Cyril Connolly

The piers are pummelled by the waves;
In a lonely field the rain
Lashes an abandoned train;
Outlaws fill the mountain caves.

Fantastic grow the evening gowns;
Agents of the Fisc pursue
Absconding tax-defaulters through
The sewers of provincial towns.

Private rites of magic send
The temple prostitutes to sleep;
All the literati keep
An imaginary friend.

Cerebrotonic Cato may
Extol the Ancient Disciplines,
But the muscle-bound Marines
Mutiny for food and pay.

Caesar's double-bed is warm
As an unimportant clerk
Writes I DO NOT LIKE MY WORK
On a pink official form.

Unendowed with wealth or pity,
Little birds with scarlet legs,
Sitting on their speckled eggs,
Eye each flu-infected city.

Altogether elsewhere, vast
Herds of reindeer move across
Miles and miles of golden moss,
Silently and very fast.

Inversnaid

This darksome burn, horseback brown,
His rollrock highroad roaring down,
In coop and in comb the fleece of his foam
Flutes and low to the lake falls home.

A windpuff-bonnet of fáwn-fróth
Turns and twindles over the broth
Of a pool so pitchblack, féll frówning,
It rounds and rounds Despair to drowning.

Degged with dew, dappled with dew
Are the groins of the braes that the brook treads
    through,
Wiry heathpacks, flitches of fern,
And the beadbonny ash that sits over the burn.

What would the world be, once bereft
Of wet and of wildness? Let them be left,
O let them be left, wildness and wet;
Long live the weeds and the wilderness yet.

He Hears the Cry of the Sedge

I wander by the edge
Of this desolate lake
Where wind cries in the sedge:
Until the axle break
That keeps the stars in their round,
And hands hurl in the deep
The banners of East and West,
And the girdle of light is unbound,
Your breast will not lie by the breast
Of your beloved in sleep.

Lines for an Old Man

The tiger in the tiger-pit
Is not more irritable than I.
The whipping tail is not more still
Than when I smell the enemy
Writhing in the essential blood
Or dangling from the friendly tree.
When I lay bare the tooth of wit
The hissing over the archèd tongue
Is more affectionate than hate,
More bitter than the love of youth,
And inaccessible by the young.
Reflected from my golden eye
The dullard knows that he is mad.

Tell me if I am not glad!

Donal Og

It is late last night the dog was speaking of you;
the snipe was speaking of you in her deep marsh.
It is you are the lonely bird through the woods;
and that you may be without a mate until you find me.

You promised me, and you said a lie to me,
that you would be before me where the sheep are
    flocked;
I gave a whistle and three hundred cries to you,
and I found nothing there but a bleating lamb.

You promised me a thing that was hard for you,
a ship of gold under a silver mast;
twelve towns with a market in all of them,
and a fine white court by the side of the sea.

You promised me a thing that is not possible,
that you would give me gloves of the skin of a fish;
that you would give me shoes of the skin of a bird;
and a suit of the dearest silk in Ireland.

When I go by myself to the Well of Loneliness,
I sit down and I go through my trouble;
when I see the world and do not see my boy,
he that has an amber shade in his hair.

It was on that Sunday I gave my love to you;
the Sunday that is last before Easter Sunday.
And myself on my knees reading the Passion;
and my two eyes giving love to you for ever.

My mother said to me not to be talking with you today,
or tomorrow, or on the Sunday;
it was a bad time she took for telling me that;
it was shutting the door after the house was robbed.

My heart is as black as the blackness of the sloe,
or as the black coal that is on the smith's forge;
or as the sole of a shoe left in white halls;
it was you put that darkness over my life.

You have taken the east from me; you have taken the
    west from me;
you have taken what is before me and what is behind
    me;
you have taken the moon, you have taken the sun from
    me;
and my fear is great that you have taken God from me!

translated from the Irish by Lady Augusta Gregory

Upon Westminster Bridge

Composed upon Westminster Bridge
September 3, 1802

Earth has not anything to show more fair:
Dull would he be of soul who could pass by
A sight so touching in its majesty:
This City now doth, like a garment, wear
The beauty of the morning; silent, bare,
Ships, towers, domes, theatres, and temples lie
Open unto the fields, and to the sky;
All bright and glittering in the smokeless air.
Never did sun more beautifully steep
In his first splendour, valley, rock, or hill;
Ne'er saw I, never felt, a calm so deep!
The river glideth at his own sweet will:
Dear God! the very houses seem asleep;
And all that mighty heart is lying still!

from An Epistle to Dr Arbuthnot

Let *Sporus* tremble – 'What? that Thing of silk,
Sporus, that mere white Curd of Ass's milk?
Satire or Sense alas! can *Sporus* feel?
Who breaks a Butterfly upon a Wheel?'
Yet let me flap this Bug with gilded wings,
This painted Child of Dirt that stinks and stings;
Whose Buzz the Witty and the Fair annoys,
Yet Wit ne'er tastes, and Beauty ne'er enjoys,
So well-bred Spaniels civilly delight
In mumbling of the Game they dare not bite.
Eternal Smiles his Emptiness betray,
As shallow streams run dimpling all the way.
Whether in florid Impotence he speaks,
And, as the Prompter breathes, the Puppet squeaks;
Or at the Ear of *Eve*, familiar Toad,
Half Froth, half Venom, spits himself abroad,
In Puns, or Politicks, or Tales, or Lyes,
Or Spite, or Smut, or Rymes, or Blasphemies.
His Wit all see-saw between *that* and *this*,
Now high, now low, now Master up, now Miss,
And he himself one vile Antithesis.
Amphibious Thing! that acting either Part,
The trifling Head, or the corrupted Heart!
Fop at the Toilet, Flatt'rer at the Board,
Now trips a Lady, and now struts a Lord.
Eve's Tempter thus the Rabbins have exprest,
A Cherub's face, a Reptile all the rest;
Beauty that shocks you, Parts that none will trust,
Wit that can creep, and Pride that licks the dust.

How to Kill

Under the parabola of a ball,
a child turning into a man,
I looked into the air too long.
The ball fell in my hand, it sang
in the closed fist: *Open Open*
Behold a gift designed to kill.

Now in my dial of glass appears
the soldier who is going to die.
He smiles, and moves about in ways
his mother knows, habits of his.
The wires touch his face: I cry
NOW. Death, like a familiar, hears

and look, has made a man of dust
of a man of flesh. This sorcery
I do. Being damned, I am amused
to see the centre of love diffused
and the waves of love travel into vacancy.
How easy it is to make a ghost.

The weightless mosquito touches
her tiny shadow on the stone,
and with how like, how infinite
a lightness, man and shadow meet.
They fuse. A shadow is a man
when the mosquito death approaches.

Anthem for Doomed Youth

What passing-bells for these who die as cattle?
   Only the monstrous anger of the guns.
   Only the stuttering rifles' rapid rattle
Can patter out their hasty orisons.
No mockeries now for them; no prayers or bells,
   Nor any voice of mourning save the choirs, –
The shrill, demented choirs of wailing shells;
   And bugles calling for them from sad shires.

What candles may be held to speed them all?
   Not in the hands of boys, but in their eyes
Shall shine the holy glimmers of good-byes.
   The pallor of girls' brows shall be their pall;
Their flowers the tenderness of silent minds,
And each slow dusk a drawing-down of blinds.

The Combe

The Combe was ever dark, ancient and dark.
Its mouth is stopped with bramble, thorn, and briar;
And no one scrambles over the sliding chalk
By beech and yew and perishing juniper
Down the half precipices of its sides, with roots
And rabbit holes for steps. The sun of Winter,
The moon of Summer, and all the singing birds
Except the missel-thrush that loves juniper,
Are quite shut out. But far more ancient and dark
The Combe looks since they killed the badger there,
Dug him out and gave him to the hounds,
That most ancient Briton of English beasts.

On the Late Massacre in Piedmont

Avenge O Lord thy slaughter'd saints, whose bones
  Lie scatter'd on the Alpine mountains cold,
  Ev'n them who kept thy truth so pure of old
  When all our fathers worship't stocks and stones,
Forget not: in thy book record their groans
  Who were thy sheep and in their ancient fold
  Slain by the bloody Piedmontese that roll'd
  Mother with infant down the rocks. Their moans
The vales redoubl'd to the hills, and they
  To Heav'n. Their martyr'd blood and ashes sow
  O'er all th'Italian fields where still doth sway
The triple tyrant: that from these may grow
  A hundredfold, who having learnt thy way
  Early may fly the Babylonian woe.

Here

I am a man now.
Pass your hand over my brow,
You can feel the place where the brains grow.

I am like a tree,
From my top boughs I can see
The footprints that led up to me.

There is blood in my veins
That has run clear of the stain
Contracted in so many loins.

Why, then, are my hands red
With the blood of so many dead?
Is this where I was misled?

Why are my hands this way
That they will not do as I say?
Does no God hear when I pray?

I have nowhere to go.
The swift satellites show
The clock of my whole being is slow.

It is too late to depart
For destinations not of the heart.
I must stay here with my hurt.

Meditation on the A30

A man on his own in a car
    Is revenging himself on his wife;
He opens the throttle and bubbles with dottle
    And puffs at his pitiful life.

'She's losing her looks very fast,
    She loses her temper all day;
That lorry won't let me get past,
    This Mini is blocking my way.

'Why can't you step on it and shift her!
    I can't go on crawling like this!
At breakfast she said that she wished I was dead –
    Thank heavens we don't have to kiss.

'I'd like a nice blonde on my knee
    And one who won't argue or nag.
Who dares to come hooting at *me*?
    I only give way to a Jag.

'You're barmy or plastered, I'll pass you, you
      bastard –
    I *will* overtake you. I *will*!'
As he clenches his pipe, his moment is ripe
    And the corner's accepting its kill.

The Tyger

Tyger! Tyger! burning bright
In the forests of the night,
What immortal hand or eye
Could frame thy fearful symmetry?

In what distant deeps or skies
Burnt the fire of thine eyes?
On what wings dare he aspire?
What the hand dare sieze the fire?

And what shoulder, & what art,
Could twist the sinews of thy heart?
And when thy heart began to beat,
What dread hand? & what dread feet?

What the hammer? what the chain?
In what furnace was thy brain?
What the anvil? what dread grasp
Dare its deadly terrors clasp?

When the stars threw down their spears,
And water'd heaven with their tears,
Did he smile his work to see?
Did he who made the Lamb make thee?

Tyger! Tyger! burning bright
In the forests of the night,
What immortal hand or eye
Dare frame thy fearful symmetry?

On First Looking into Chapman's Homer

Much have I travelled in the realms of gold,
    And many goodly states and kingdoms seen;
    Round many western islands have I been
Which bards in fealty to Apollo hold.
Oft of one wide expanse had I been told
    That deep-browed Homer ruled as his demesne;
    Yet did I never breathe its pure serene
Till I heard Chapman speak out loud and bold:
Then felt I like some watcher of the skies
    When a new planet swims into his ken;
Or like stout Cortez when with eagle eyes
    He stared at the Pacific – and all his men
Looked at each other with a wild surmise –
    Silent, upon a peak in Darien.

Ozymandias

I met a traveler from an antique land
Who said: Two vast and trunkless legs of stone
Stand in the desert . . . Near them, on the sand,
Half sunk, a shattered visage lies, whose frown,
And wrinkled lip, and sneer of cold command,
Tell that its sculptor well those passions read
Which yet survive, stamped on these lifeless things,
The hand that mocked them, and the heart that fed:
And on the pedestal these words appear:
'My name is Ozymandias, king of kings:
Look on my works, ye Mighty, and despair!'
Nothing beside remains. Round the decay
Of that colossal wreck, boundless and bare
The lone and level sands stretch far away.

'Like Rain it sounded till it curved'

Like Rain it sounded till it curved
And then I knew 'twas Wind –
It walked as wet as any Wave
But swept as dry as sand –
When it had pushed itself away
To some remotest Plain
A coming as of Hosts was heard
That was indeed the Rain –
It filled the Wells, it pleased the Pools
It warbled in the Road –
It pulled the spigot from the Hills
And let the Floods abroad –
It loosened acres, lifted seas
The sites of Centres stirred
Then like Elijah rode away
Upon a Wheel of Cloud.

Mad Tom's Song

From the hag and hungry goblin
    That into rags would rend ye
The spirit that stands by the naked man
    In the book of moons defend ye,
That of your five sound senses
    Ye never be forsaken
Nor wander from yourselves with Tom
    Abroad to beg your bacon.
        While I do sing: 'Any food, any feeding,
        Feeding, drink, or clothing?
        Come dame, or maid, be not afraid,
        Poor Tom will injure nothing.'

Of thirty bare yeares have I
    Twice twenty been enraged,
And of forty been thrice times fifteen
    In durance soundly caged.
On the lordly lofts of bedlam
    With stubble soft and dainty,
Brave bracelets strong, sweet whips ding-dong,
    And wholesome hunger plenty,
        While I do sing, etc.

A thought I took for Maudline
    In a cruse of cockle pottage
With a thing thus tall – God bless you all
    I befell into this dotage.
I've slept not since the Conquest,
    Ere then I never waked
Till the roguish fay of love where I lay

Me found and stripped me naked.
　　While I do sing, etc.

When I short have shorn my sow's face
　　And snigged my hairy barrel
At an oaken inn I pound my skin
　　In a suit of gay apparel.
The moon's my constant mistress
　　And the lovely owl my marrow
The flaming drake and the night-crow make
　　Me music to my sorrow.
　　While I do sing, etc.

The palsy plague my pulses
　　If I prig your pigs or pullen,
Your culvers take, or matchless make
　　Your chanticleer or solan!
When I want provant, with Humphry
　　I sup and when benighted
I repose in Paul's with walking souls
　　And never am affrighted.
　　While I do sing, etc.

I know more than Apollo
　　For oft when he lies sleeping
I see the stars at bloody wars
　　And the wounded welkin weeping,
The moon embrace her shepherd,
　　And the Queen of Love her warrior,
When the first doth horn the start of the morn
　　And the next the heavenly farrier.
　　While I do sing, etc.

The gypsies Snap and Pedro
　　Are none of Tom's camradoes.

[29]

The punk I scorn, and cut-purse sworn
    And the roaring-boy's bravadoes.
The meek, the white, the gentle
    Me handle, touch and spare not,
But those that cross Tom Rhinoceros
    Do what the panther dare not.
        While I do sing, etc.

With an host of furious fancies
    Whereof I am commander
With a burning spear and a horse of air
    To the wilderness I wander.
By a knight of ghosts and shadows
    I summoned am to tourney
Ten leagues beyond the wide world's end
    Methinks it is no journey.
        While I do sing, etc.

I'll bark against the dog-star
    I'll crow away the morning
I'll chase the moon till it be noon
    And make her leave her horning,
But I'll find merry mad Maudline
    And seek whate'er betides her,
And I will love beneath or above
    The dirty earth that hides her.
        While I do sing, etc.

version by Robert Graves

Jabberwocky

'Twas brillig, and the slithy toves
    Did gyre and gimble in the wabe:
All mimsy were the borogroves,
    And the mome raths outgrabe.

'Beware the Jabberwock, my son!
    The jaws that bite, the claws that catch!
Beware the Jubjub bird, and shun
    The frumious Bandersnatch!'

He took his vorpal sword in hand:
    Long time the manxome foe he sought –
So rested he by the Tumtum tree,
    And stood awhile in thought.

And, as in uffish thought he stood,
    The Jabberwock, with eyes of flame,
Came whiffling through the tulgey wood,
    And burbled as it came!

One, two! One, two! And through and through
    The vorpal blade went snicker-snack!
He left it dead, and with its head
    He went galumphing back.

'And hast thou slain the Jabberwock?
    Come to my arms, my beamish boy!
O frabjous day! Callooh! Callay!'
    He chortled in his joy.

'Twas brillig, and the slithy toves
　　Did gyre and gimble in the wabe:
All mimsy were the borogroves,
　　And the mome raths outgrabe.

ANDREW YOUNG

Field-Glasses

Though buds still speak in hints
And frozen ground has set the flints
As fast as precious stones
And birds perch on the boughs, silent as cones,

Suddenly waked from sloth
Young trees put on a ten years' growth
And stones double their size,
Drawn nearer through field-glasses' greater eyes.

Why I borrow their sight
Is not to give small birds a fright
Creeping up close by inches;
I make the trees come, bringing tits and finches.

I lift a field itself
As lightly as I might a shelf,
And the rooks do not rage
Caught for a moment in my crystal cage.

And while I stand and look,
Their private lives an open book,
I feel so privileged
My shoulders prick, as though they were half-fledged.

WALTER DE LA MARE

An Epitaph

Here lies a most beautiful lady,
Light of step and heart was she;
I think she was the most beautiful lady
That ever was in the West Country.

But beauty vanishes; beauty passes;
However rare – rare it be;
And when I crumble, who will remember
This lady of the West Country?

'My mistress' eyes are nothing like the sun'

My mistress' eyes are nothing like the sun:
Coral is far more red than her lips' red:
If snow be white, why then her breasts are dun:
If hairs be wires, black wires grow on her head.
I have seen roses damask'd, red and white.
But no such roses see I in her cheeks:
And in some perfumes is there more delight
Than in the breath that from my mistress reeks.
I love to hear her speak, yet well I know
That music hath a far more pleasing sound:
I grant I never saw a goddess go, –
My mistress, when she walks, treads on the ground:
    And yet, by heaven, I think my love as rare
    As any she belied with false compare.

La Figlia Che Piange

O quam te memorem virgo . . .

Stand on the highest pavement of the stair –
Lean on a garden urn –
Weave, weave the sunlight in your hair –
Clasp your flowers to you with a pained surprise –
Fling them to the ground and turn
With a fugitive resentment in your eyes:
But weave, weave the sunlight in your hair.

So I would have had him leave,
So I would have had her stand and grieve,
So he would have left
As the soul leaves the body torn and bruised,
As the mind deserts the body it has used.
I should find
Some way incomparably light and deft,
Some way we both should understand,
Simple and faithless as a smile and shake of the hand.

She turned away, but with the autumn weather
Compelled my imagination many days,
Many days and many hours:
Her hair over her arms and her arms full of flowers.
And I wonder how they should have been together!
I should have lost a gesture and a pose.
Sometimes these cogitations still amaze
The troubled midnight and the noon's repose.

Provide, Provide

The witch that came (the withered hag)
To wash the steps with pail and rag
Was once the beauty Abishag,

The picture pride of Hollywood.
Too many fall from great and good
For you to doubt the likelihood.

Die early and avoid the fate.
Or if predestined to die late,
Make up your mind to die in state.

Make the whole stock exchange your own!
If need be occupy a throne,
Where nobody can call *you* crone.

Some have relied on what they knew,
Others on being simply true.
What worked for them might work for you.

No memory of having starred
Atones for later disregard
Or keeps the end from being hard.

Better to go down dignified
With boughten friendship at your side
Than none at all. Provide, provide!

La Belle Dame sans Merci

O what can ail thee, knight-at-arms,
    Alone and palely loitering?
The sedge has withered from the lake,
    And no birds sing.

O what can ail thee, knight-at-arms,
    So haggard and so woe-begone?
The squirrel's granary is full,
    And the harvest's done.

I see a lily on thy brow,
    With anguish moist and fever-dew,
And on thy cheeks a fading rose
    Fast withereth too.

I met a lady in the meads,
    Full beautiful – a faery's child,
Her hair was long, her foot was light,
    And her eyes were wild.

I made a garland for her head,
    And bracelets too, and fragrant zone;
She looked at me as she did love,
    And made sweet moan.

I set her on my pacing steed,
    And nothing else saw all day long,
For sidelong would she bend, and sing
    A faery's song.

She found me roots of relish sweet,
    And honey wild, and manna-dew,

And sure in language strange she said –
    'I love thee true'.

She took me to her elfin grot,
    And there she wept and sighed full sore,
And there I shut her wild wild eyes
    With kisses four.

And there she lullèd me asleep
    And there I dreamed – Ah! woe betide! –
The latest dream I ever dreamt
    On the cold hill side.

I saw pale kings and princes too,
    Pale warriors, death-pale were they all;
They cried – 'La Belle Dame sans Merci
    Thee hath in thrall!'

I saw their starved lips in the gloam,
    With horrid warning gapèd wide,
And I awoke and found me here,
    On the cold hill's side.

And this is why I sojourn here
    Alone and palely loitering,
Though the sedge is withered from the lake,
    And no birds sing.

Piano

Softly, in the dusk, a woman is singing to me;
Taking me back down the vista of years, till I see
A child sitting under the piano, in the boom of the
    tingling strings
And pressing the small, poised feet of a mother who
    smiles as she sings.

In spite of myself, the insidious mastery of song
Betrays me back, till the heart of me weeps to belong
To the old Sunday evenings at home, with winter
    outside
And hymns in the cosy parlour, the tinkling piano our
    guide.

So now it is vain for the singer to burst into clamour
With the great black piano appassionato. The glamour
Of childish days is upon me, my manhood is cast
Down in the flood of remembrance, I weep like a child for
    the past.

The Solitary Reaper

Behold her, single in the field,
Yon solitary Highland Lass!
Reaping and singing by herself;
Stop here, or gently pass!
Alone she cuts and binds the grain,
And sings a melancholy strain;
O listen! for the Vale profound
Is overflowing with the sound.

No Nightingale did ever chaunt
More welcome notes to weary bands
Of travellers in some shady haunt,
Among Arabian sands:
A voice so thrilling ne'er was heard
In spring-time from the Cuckoo-bird,
Breaking the silence of the seas
Among the farthest Hebrides.

Will no one tell me what she sings? –
Perhaps the plaintive numbers flow
For old, unhappy, far-off things,
And battles long ago:
Or is it some more humble lay,
Familiar matter of today?
Some natural sorrow, loss, or pain,
That has been, and may be again?

Whate'er the theme, the Maiden sang
As if her song could have no ending;
I saw her singing at her work,
And o'er the sickle bending; –

I listened, motionless and still;
And, as I mounted up the hill,
The music in my heart I bore,
Long after it was heard no more.

Kubla Khan

In Xanadu did Kubla Khan
A stately pleasure-dome decree:
Where Alph, the sacred river, ran
Through caverns measureless to man
   Down to a sunless sea.
So twice five miles of fertile ground
With walls and towers were girdled round:
And there were gardens bright with sinuous rills,
Where blossomed many an incense-bearing tree;
And here were forests ancient as the hills,
Enfolding sunny spots of greenery.

But oh! that deep romantic chasm which slanted
Down the green hill athwart a cedarn cover!
A savage place! as holy and enchanted
As e'er beneath a waning moon was haunted
By woman wailing for her demon-lover!
   And from this chasm, with ceaseless turmoil seething,
As if this earth in fast thick pants were breathing,
A mighty fountain momently was forced:
Amid whose swift half-intermitted burst
Huge fragments vaulted like rebounding hail,
Or chaffy grain beneath the thresher's flail:
And 'mid these dancing rocks at once and ever
It flung up momently the sacred river.
Five miles meandering with a mazy motion
Through wood and dale the sacred river ran,
Then reached the caverns measureless to man,
And sank in tumult to a lifeless ocean:
And 'mid the tumult Kubla heard from far

Ancestral voices prophesying war!
   The shadow of the dome of pleasure
   Floated midway on the waves;
   Where was heard the mingled measure
   From the fountain and the caves.
It was a miracle of rare device,
A sunny pleasure-dome with caves of ice!

   A damsel with a dulcimer
   In a vision once I saw:
   It was an Abyssinian maid,
   And on her dulcimer she played,
   Singing of Mount Abora.
   Could I revive within me
   Her symphony and song,
   To such a deep delight 'twould win me,
That with music loud and long,
I would build that dome in air,
That sunny dome! those caves of ice!
And all who heard should see them there,
And all should cry, Beware! Beware!
His flashing eyes, his floating hair!
Weave a circle round him thrice,
And close your eyes with holy dread,
For he on honey-dew hath fed,
And drunk the milk of Paradise.

Marina

Quis hic locus, quae
regio, quae mundi plaga?

What seas what shores what grey rocks and what islands
What water lapping the bow
And scent of pine and the woodthrush singing through the
    fog
What images return
O my daughter.

Those who sharpen the tooth of the dog, meaning
Death
Those who glitter with the glory of the hummingbird,
    meaning
Death
Those who sit in the sty of contentment, meaning
Death
Those who suffer the ecstasy of the animals, meaning
Death

Are become unsubstantial, reduced by a wind,
A breath of pine, and the woodsong fog
By this grace dissolved in place

What is this face, less clear and clearer
The pulse in the arm, less strong and stronger –
Given or lent? more distant than stars and nearer than the
    eye

Whispers and small laughter between leaves and
    hurrying feet
Under sleep, where all the waters meet.

Bowsprit cracked with ice and paint cracked with
    heat.
I made this, I have forgotten
And remember.
The rigging weak and the canvas rotten
Between one June and another September.
Made this unknowing, half conscious, unknown, my
    own.
The garboard strake leaks, the seams need caulking.
This form, this face, this life
Living to live in a world of time beyond me; let me
Resign my life for this life, my speech for that unspoken,
The awakened, lips parted, the hope, the new ships.

What seas what shores what granite islands towards
    my timbers
And woodthrush calling through the fog
My daughter.

'A woman's beauty is like a white'

A woman's beauty is like a white
Frail bird, like a white sea-bird alone
At daybreak after stormy night
Between two furrows upon the ploughed land:
A sudden storm, and it was thrown
Between dark furrows upon the ploughed land.
How many centuries spent
The sedentary soul
In toils of measurement
Beyond eagle or mole,
Beyond hearing or seeing,
Or Archimedes' guess,
To raise into being
That loveliness?

A strange, unserviceable thing,
A fragile, exquisite, pale shell,
That the vast troubled waters bring
To the loud sands before day has broken.
The storm arose and suddenly fell
Amid the dark before day had broken.
What death? what discipline?
What bonds no man could unbind,
Being imagined within
The labyrinth of the mind,
What pursuing or fleeing,
What wounds, what bloody press,
Dragged into being
This loveliness?

Song for the Clatter-Bones

God rest that wicked woman,
Queen Jezebel, the bitch
Who peeled the clothes from her shoulder-bones
Down to her spent teats
As she stretched out of the window
Among the geraniums, where
She chaffed and laughed like one half daft
Titivating her painted hair –

King Jehu he drove to her,
She tipped him a fancy beck;
But he from his knacky side-car spoke,
'Who'll break that dewlapped neck?'
And so she was thrown from the window;
Like Lucifer she fell
Beneath the feet of the horses and they beat
The light out of Jezebel.

That corpse wasn't planted in clover;
Ah, nothing of her was found
Save those grey bones that Hare-foot Mike
Gave me for their lovely sound;
And as once her dancing body
Made star-lit princes sweat,
So I'll just clack: though her ghost lacks a back
There's music in the old bones yet.

A Subaltern's Love-song

Miss J. Hunter Dunn, Miss J. Hunter Dunn,
Furnish'd and burnish'd by Aldershot sun,
What strenuous singles we played after tea,
We in the tournament – you against me!

Love-thirty, love-forty, oh! weakness of joy,
The speed of a swallow, the grace of a boy,
With carefullest carelessness, gaily you won,
I am weak from your loveliness, Joan Hunter Dunn.

Miss Joan Hunter Dunn, Miss Joan Hunter Dunn,
How mad I am, sad I am, glad that you won.
The warm-handled racket is back in its press,
But my shock-headed victor, she loves me no less.

Her father's euonymus shines as we walk,
And swing past the summer-house, buried in talk,
And cool the verandah that welcomes us in
To the six-o'clock news and a lime-juice and gin.

The scent of the conifers, sound of the bath,
The view from my bedroom of moss-dappled path,
As I struggle with double-end evening tie,
For we dance at the Golf Club, my victor and I.

On the floor of her bedroom lie blazer and shorts
And the cream-coloured walls are be-trophied with sports,
And westering, questioning settles the sun
On your low-leaded window, Miss Joan Hunter Dunn.

The Hillman is waiting, the light's in the hall,
The pictures of Egypt are bright on the wall,

My sweet, I am standing beside the oak stair
And there on the landing's the light on your hair.

By roads 'not adopted', by woodlanded ways,
She drove to the club in the late summer haze,
Into nine-o'clock Camberley, heavy with bells
And mushroomy, pine-woody, evergreen smells.

Miss Joan Hunter Dunn, Miss Joan Hunter Dunn,
I can hear from the car-park the dance has begun.
Oh! full Surrey twilight! importunate band!
Oh! strongly adorable tennis-girl's hand!

Around us are Rovers and Austins afar,
Above us, the intimate roof of the car,
And here on my right is the girl of my choice,
With the tilt of her nose and the chime of her voice,

And the scent of her wrap, and the words never said,
And the ominous, ominous dancing ahead.
We sat in the car-park till twenty to one
And now I'm engaged to Miss Joan Hunter Dunn.

'Other slow arts entirely keep the brain'

Other slow arts entirely keep the brain,
And therefore, finding barren practisers,
Scarce show a harvest of their heavy toil;
But love, first learned in a lady's eyes,
Lives not alone immured in the brain,
But, with the motion of all elements,
Courses as swift as thought in every power,
And gives to every power a double power,
Above their functions and their offices.
It adds a precious seeing to the eye;
A lover's eyes will gaze an eagle blind;
A lover's ear will hear the lowest sound,
When the suspicious head of theft is stopp'd:
Love's feeling is more soft and sensible
Than are the tender horns of cockled snails:
Love's tongue proves dainty Bacchus gross in taste.
For valour, is not Love a Hercules,
Still climbing trees in the Hesperides?
Subtle as Sphinx; as sweet and musical
As bright Apollo's lute, strung with his hair;
And when Love speaks, the voice of all the gods
Makes heaven drowsy with the harmony.

Long John Brown and Little Mary Bell

Little Mary Bell had a Fairy in a Nut,
Long John Brown had the Devil in his Gut;
Long John Brown lov'd Little Mary Bell,
And the Fairy drew the Devil into the Nut-shell.

Her Fairy Skip'd out and her Fairy Skip'd in;
He laugh'd at the Devil saying 'Love is a Sin.'
The Devil he raged and the Devil he was wroth,
And the Devil enter'd into the Young Man's broth.

He was soon in the Gut of the loving Young Swain,
For John eat and drank to drive away Love's pain;
But all he could do he grew thinner and thinner,
Tho' he eat and drank as much as ten Men for his dinner.

Some said he had a Wolf in his stomach day and night,
Some said he had the Devil and they guess'd right;
The Fairy skip'd about in his Glory, Joy and Pride,
And he laugh'd at the Devil till poor John Brown died.

Then the Fairy skip'd out of the old Nut-shell,
And woe and alack for Pretty Mary Bell!
For the Devil crept in when the Fairy skip'd out,
And there goes Miss Bell with her fusty old Nut.

Spring and Fall

to a young child

Márgarét, áre you gríeving
Over Goldengrove unleaving?
Leáves, líke the things of man, you
With your fresh thoughts care for, can you?
Áh! ás the heart grows older
It will come to such sights colder
By and by, nor spare a sigh
Though worlds of wanwood leafmeal lie;
And yet you *will* weep and know why.
Now no matter, child, the name:
Sórrow's spríngs áre the same.
Nor mouth had, no nor mind, expressed
What heart heard of, ghost guessed:
It ís the blight man was born for,
It is Margaret you mourn for.

'They flee from me, that sometime did me seek'

They flee from me, that sometime did me seek
With naked foot stalking in my chamber.
I have seen them gentle, tame, and meek
That now are wild, and do not remember
That sometime they put themself in danger
To take bread at my hand; and now they range,
Busily seeking with a continual change.

Thanked be fortune it hath been otherwise
Twenty times better, but once in special,
In thin array after a pleasant guise
When her loose gown from her shoulders did fall,
And she me caught in her arms long and small,
Therewithal sweetly did me kiss,
And softly said, 'Dear heart, how like you this?'

It was no dream: I lay broad waking
But all is turned thorough my gentleness
Into a strange fashion of forsaking,
And I have leave to go of her goodness,
And she also to use newfangleness.
But since that I so kindly am served,
I would fain know what she hath deserved.

'Fear no more the heat o' the sun'

Fear no more the heat o' the sun,
   Nor the furious winter's rages;
Thou thy worldly task hast done,
   Home art gone, and ta'en thy wages;
Golden lads and girls all must
   As chimney-sweepers, come to dust.

Fear no more the frown o' the great,
   Thou art past the tyrant's stroke:
Care no more to clothe and eat;
   To thee the reed is as the oak;
The sceptre, learning, physic, must
   All follow this, and come to dust.

Fear no more the lightning-flash,
   Nor the all-dreaded thunder-stone:
Fear not slander, censure rash;
   Thou hast finish'd joy and moan:
All lovers young, all lovers must
   Consign to thee, and come to dust.

No exorcizer harm thee!
   Nor no witchcraft charm thee!
Ghost unlaid forbear thee!
   Nothing ill come near thee!
Quiet consummation have:
   And renowned be thy grave!

'Stop all the clocks, cut off the telephone'

Stop all the clocks, cut off the telephone,
Prevent the dog from barking with a juicy bone,
Silence the pianos and with muffled drum
Bring out the coffin, let the mourners come.

Let aeroplanes circle moaning overhead
Scribbling on the sky the message He Is Dead,
Put crêpe bows round the white necks of the public doves,
Let the traffic policemen wear black cotton gloves.

He was my North, my South, my East and West,
My working week and my Sunday rest,
My noon, my midnight, my talk, my song;
I thought that love would last for ever: I was wrong.

The stars are not wanted now: put out every one;
Pack up the moon and dismantle the sun;
Pour away the ocean and sweep up the wood;
For nothing now can ever come to any good.

The Smile

There is a Smile of Love,
And there is a Smile of Deceit,
And there is a Smile of Smiles
In which these two Smiles meet.

And there is a Frown of Hate,
And there is a Frown of Disdain,
And there is a Frown of Frowns
Which you strive to forget in vain,

For it sticks in the Heart's deep Core
And it sticks in the deep Back bone;
And no Smile that ever was smil'd,
But only one Smile alone,

That betwixt the Cradle & Grave
It only once Smil'd can be;
But, when it once is Smil'd,
There's an end to all Misery.

Blue Girls

Twirling your blue skirts, travelling the sward
Under the towers of your seminary,
Go listen to your teachers old and contrary
Without believing a word.

Tie the white fillets then about your hair
And think no more of what will come to pass
Than bluebirds that go walking on the grass
And chattering on the air.

Practise your beauty, blue girls, before it fail;
And I will cry with my loud lips and publish
Beauty which all our power shall never establish,
It is so frail.

For I could tell you a story which is true;
I know a woman with a terrible tongue,
Blear eyes fallen from blue,
All her perfections tarnished – yet it is not long
Since she was lovelier than any of you.

The Relique

When my grave is broke up again
Some second guest to entertain,
(For graves have learn'd that woman-head
To be to more than one a Bed)
    And he that digs it, spies
A bracelet of bright hair about the bone,
    Will he not let'us alone,
And think that there a loving couple lies,
Who thought that this device might be some way
To make their souls, at the last busy day,
Meet at this grave, and make a little stay?

If this fall in a time, or land,
Where mis-devotion doth command,
Then, he that digs us up, will bring
Us, to the Bishop, and the King,
    To make us Reliques; then
Thou shalt be a Mary Magdalen, and I
    A something else thereby;
All women shall adore us, and some men;
And since at such time, miracles are sought,
I would have that age by this paper taught
What miracles we harmless lovers wrought.

First, we lov'd well and faithfully,
Yet knew not what we lov'd, nor why,
Difference of sex no more we knew,
Than our Guardian Angels do;
    Coming and going, we
Perchance might kiss, but not between those meals;

Our hands ne'r touched the seals,
Which nature, injur'd by late law, sets free:
These miracles we did; but now alas,
All measure, and all language, I should pass,
Should I tell what a miracle she was.

A Refusal to Mourn the Death, by Fire, of a Child in London

Never until the mankind making
Bird beast and flower
Fathering and all humbling darkness
Tells with silence the last light breaking
And the still hour
Is come of the sea tumbling in harness

And I must enter again the round
Zion of the water bead
And the synagogue of the ear of corn
Shall I let pray the shadow of a sound
Or sow my salt seed
In the least valley of sackcloth to mourn

The majesty and burning of the child's death.
I shall not murder
The mankind of her going with a grave truth
Nor blaspheme down the stations of the breath
With any further
Elegy of innocence and youth.

Deep with the first dead lies London's daughter,
Robed in the long friends,
The grains beyond age, the dark veins of her mother,
Secret by the unmourning water
Of the riding Thames.
After the first death, there is no other.

The Return

See, they return; ah, see the tentative
      Movements, and the slow feet,
      The trouble in the pace and the uncertain
      Wavering!

See, they return, one, and by one,
With fear, as half-awakened;
As if the snow should hesitate
And murmur in the wind,
      and half turn back;
These were the 'Wing'd-with-Awe,'
      Inviolable,

Gods of the wingèd shoe!
With them the silver hounds,
      sniffing the trace of air!

Haie! Haie!
    These were the swift to harry;
These the keen-scented;
These were the souls of blood.

Slow on the leash,
      pallid the leash-men!

The Skunk

Up, black, striped and damasked like the chasuble
At a funeral mass, the skunk's tail
Paraded the skunk. Night after night
I expected her like a visitor.

The refrigerator whinnied into silence.
My desk light softened beyond the veranda.
Small oranges loomed in the orange tree.
I began to be tense as a voyeur.

After eleven years I was composing
Love-letters again, broaching the word 'wife'
Like a stored cask, as if its slender vowel
Had mutated into the night earth and air

Of California. The beautiful, useless
Tang of eucalyptus spelt your absence.
The aftermath of a mouthful of wine
Was like inhaling you off a cold pillow.

And there she was, the intent and glamorous,
Ordinary, mysterious skunk,
Mythologized, demythologized,
Snuffing the boards five feet beyond me.

It all came back to me last night, stirred
By the sootfall of your things at bedtime,
Your head-down, tail-up hunt in a bottom drawer
For the black plunge-line nightdress.

'That time of year thou mayst in me behold'

That time of year thou mayst in me behold
When yellow leaves, or none, or few, do hang
Upon those boughs which shake against the cold,
Bare ruin'd choirs, where late the sweet birds sang.
In me thou see'st the twilight of such day
As after sunset fadeth in the west;
Which by and by black night doth take away,
Death's second self, that seals up all in rest.
In me thou see'st the glowing of such fire,
That on the ashes of his youth doth lie,
As the death-bed whereon it must expire
Consum'd with that which it was nourish'd by.
   This thou perceiv'st, which makes thy love more
      strong,
   To love that well which thou must leave ere long.

Easter 1916

I have met them at close of day
Coming with vivid faces
From counter or desk among grey
Eighteenth-century houses.
I have passed with a nod of the head
Or polite meaningless words,
Or have lingered awhile and said
Polite meaningless words,
And thought before I had done
Of a mocking tale or a gibe
To please a companion
Around the fire at the club,
Being certain that they and I
But lived where motley is worn:
All changed, changed utterly:
A terrible beauty is born.

That woman's days were spent
In ignorant good-will,
Her nights in argument
Until her voice grew shrill.
What voice more sweet than hers
When, young and beautiful,
She rode to harriers?
This man had kept a school
And rode our wingèd horse;
This other his helper and friend
Was coming into his force;
He might have won fame in the end,
So sensitive his nature seemed,

So daring and sweet his thought.
This other man I had dreamed
A drunken, vainglorious lout.
He had done most bitter wrong
To some who are near my heart,
Yet I number him in the song;
He, too, has resigned his part
In the casual comedy;
He, too, has been changed in his turn,
Transformed utterly:
A terrible beauty is born.

Hearts with one purpose alone
Through summer and winter seem
Enchanted to a stone
To trouble the living stream.
The horse that comes from the road,
The rider, the birds that range
From cloud to tumbling cloud,
Minute by minute they change;
A shadow of cloud on the stream
Changes minute by minute;
A horse-hoof slides on the brim,
And a horse plashes within it;
The long-legged moor-hens dive,
And hens to moor-cocks call;
Minute by minute they live:
The stone's in the midst of all.

Too long a sacrifice
Can make a stone of the heart.
O when may it suffice?
That is Heaven's part, our part
To murmur name upon name,

As a mother names her child
When sleep at last has come
On limbs that had run wild.
What is it but nightfall?
No, no, not night but death;
Was it needless death after all?
For England may keep faith
For all that is done and said.
We know their dream; enough
To know they dreamed and are dead;
And what if excess of love
Bewildered them till they died?
I write it out in a verse –
MacDonagh and MacBride
And Connolly and Pearse
Now and in time to be,
Wherever green is worn,
Are changed, changed utterly:
A terrible beauty is born.

Tintern Abbey

Composed a few miles above Tintern Abbey,
on revisiting the Banks of the Wye during a tour.
July 13, 1798

Five years have past; five summers, with the length
Of five long winters! and again I hear
These waters, rolling from their mountain-springs
With a soft inland murmur. – Once again
Do I behold these steep and lofty cliffs,
That on a wild secluded scene impress
Thoughts of more deep seclusion; and connect
The landscape with the quiet of the sky.
The day is come when I again repose
Here, under this dark sycamore, and view
These plots of cottage-ground, these orchard-tufts,
Which at this season, with their unripe fruits,
Are clad in one green hue, and lose themselves
'Mid groves and copses. Once again I see
These hedge-rows, hardly hedge-rows, little lines
Of sportive wood run wild: these pastoral farms,
Green to the very door; and wreaths of smoke
Sent up, in silence, from among the trees!
With some uncertain notice, as might seem
Of vagrant dwellers in the houseless woods,
Or of some Hermit's cave, where by his fire
The Hermit sits alone.

              These beauteous forms,
Through a long absence, have not been to me
As is a landscape to a blind man's eye:
But oft, in lonely rooms, and 'mid the din

Of towns and cities, I have owed to them,
In hours of weariness, sensations sweet,
Felt in the blood, and felt along the heart;
And passing even into my purer mind,
With tranquil restoration: – feelings too
Of unremembered pleasure: such, perhaps,
As have no slight or trivial influence
On that best portion of a good man's life,
His little, nameless, unremembered, acts
Of kindness and of love. Nor less, I trust,
To them I may have owed another gift,
Of aspect more sublime; that blessed mood,
In which the burthen of the mystery,
In which the heavy and the weary weight
Of all this unintelligible world,
Is lightened: – that serene and blessed mood,
In which the affections gently lead us on, –
Until, the breath of this corporeal frame
And even the motion of our human blood
Almost suspended, we are laid asleep
In body, and become a living soul:
While with an eye made quiet by the power
Of harmony, and the deep power of joy,
We see into the life of things.
                                        If this
Be but a vain belief, yet, oh! how oft –
In darkness and amid the many shapes
Of joyless daylight; when the fretful stir
Unprofitable, and the fever of the world,
Have hung upon the beatings of my heart –
How oft, in spirit, have I turned to thee,
O sylvan Wye! thou wanderer thro' the woods,
How often has my spirit turned to thee!

And now, with gleams of half-extinguished thought,
With many recognitions dim and faint,
And somewhat of a sad perplexity,
The picture of the mind revives again:
While here I stand, not only with the sense
Of present pleasure, but with pleasing thoughts
That in this moment there is life and food
For future years. And so I dare to hope,
Though changed, no doubt, from what I was when first
I came among these hills; when like a roe
I bounded o'er the mountains, by the sides
Of the deep rivers, and the lonely streams,
Wherever nature led: more like a man
Flying from something that he dreads than one
Who sought the thing he loved. For nature then
(The coarser pleasures of my boyish days,
And their glad animal movements all gone by)
To me was all in all. – I cannot paint
What then I was. The sounding cataract
Haunted me like a passion: the tall rock,
The mountain, and the deep and gloomy wood,
Their colours and their forms, were then to me
An appetite; a feeling and a love,
That had no need of a remoter charm,
By thought supplied, nor any interest
Unborrowed from the eye. – That time is past,
And all its aching joys are now no more,
And all its dizzy raptures. Not for this
Faint I, nor mourn nor murmur; other gifts
Have followed; for such loss, I would believe,
Abundant recompense. For I have learned
To look on nature, not as in the hour
Of thoughtless youth; but hearing often-times

The still, sad music of humanity,
Nor harsh nor grating, though of ample power
To chasten and subdue. And I have felt
A presence that disturbs me with the joy
Of elevated thoughts; a sense sublime
Of something far more deeply interfused,
Whose dwelling is the light of setting suns,
And the round ocean and the living air,
And the blue sky, and in the mind of man:
A motion and a spirit, that impels
All thinking things, all objects of all thought,
And rolls through all things. Therefore am I still
A lover of the meadows and the woods,
And mountains; and of all that we behold
From this green earth; of all the mighty world
Of eye, and ear, – both what they half create,
And what perceive; well pleased to recognise
In nature and the language of the sense
The anchor of my purest thoughts, the nurse,
The guide, the guardian of my heart, and soul
Of all my moral being.

              Nor perchance,
If I were not thus taught, should I the more
Suffer my genial spirits to decay:
For thou art with me here upon the banks
Of this fair river; thou my dearest Friend,
My dear, dear Friend; and in thy voice I catch
The language of my former heart, and read
My former pleasures in the shooting lights
Of thy wild eyes. Oh! yet a little while
May I behold in thee what I was once,
My dear, dear Sister! and this prayer I make,
Knowing that Nature never did betray

The heart that loved her; 'tis her privilege,
Through all the years of this our life, to lead
From joy to joy: for she can so inform
The mind that is within us, so impress
With quietness and beauty, and so feed
With lofty thoughts, that neither evil tongues,
Rash judgments, nor the sneers of selfish men,
Nor greetings where no kindness is, nor all
The dreary intercourse of daily life,
Shall e'er prevail against us, or disturb
Our cheerful faith, that all which we behold
Is full of blessings. Therefore let the moon
Shine on thee in thy solitary walk;
And let the misty mountain-winds be free
To blow against thee: and, in after years,
When these wild ecstasies shall be matured
Into a sober pleasure; when thy mind
Shall be a mansion for all lovely forms,
Thy memory be as a dwelling-place
For all sweet sounds and harmonies; oh! then,
If solitude, or fear, or pain, or grief,
Should be thy portion, with what healing thoughts
Of tender joy wilt thou remember me,
And these my exhortations! Nor, perchance –
If I should be where I no more can hear
Thy voice, nor catch from thy wild eyes these gleams
Of past existence – wilt thou, then forget
That on the banks of this delightful stream
We stood together; and that I, so long
A worshipper of Nature, hither came
Unwearied in that service: rather say
With warmer love – oh! with far deeper zeal
Of holier love. Nor wilt thou then forget

That after many wanderings, many years
Of absence, these steep woods and lofty cliffs,
And this green pastoral landscape, were to me
More dear, both for themselves and for thy sake!

The Way through the Woods

They shut the road through the woods
Seventy years ago.
Weather and rain have undone it again,
And now you would never know
There was once a road through the woods
Before they planted the trees.
It is underneath the coppice and heath
And the thin anemones.
Only the keeper sees
That, where the ring-dove broods,
And the badgers roll at ease,
There was once a road through the woods.

Yet, if you enter the woods
Of a summer evening late,
When the night-air cools on the trout-ringed pools
Where the otter whistles his mate,
(They fear not men in the woods,
Because they see so few.)
You will hear the beat of a horse's feet,
And the swish of a skirt in the dew,
Steadily cantering through
The misty solitudes,
As though they perfectly knew
The old lost road through the woods . . .
But there is no road through the woods.

Beeny Cliff

March 1870–March 1913

O the opal and the sapphire of that wandering western sea,
And the woman riding high above with bright hair
   flapping free –
The woman whom I loved so, and who loyally loved me.

The pale mews plained below us, and the waves seemed far
   away
In a nether sky, engrossed in saying their ceaseless
   babbling say,
As we laughed light-heartedly aloft on that clear-sunned
   March day.

A little cloud then cloaked us, and there flew an irised rain,
And the Atlantic dyed its levels with a dull misfeatured
   stain,
And then the sun burst out again, and purples prinked the
   main.

– Still in all its chasmal beauty bulks old Beeny to the sky,
And shall she and I not go there once again now March is
   nigh,
And the sweet things said in that March say anew there by
   and by?

What if still in chasmal beauty looms that wild weird
   western shore,
The woman now is – elsewhere – whom the ambling pony
   bore,
And nor knows nor cares for Beeny, and will laugh there
   nevermore.

The Windhover:

To Christ our Lord

I caught this morning morning's minion, king-
   dom of daylight's dauphin, dapple-dawn-drawn Falcon,
     in his riding
   Of the rolling level underneath him steady air, and
     striding
High there, how he rung upon the rein of a wimpling wing
In his ecstasy! then off, off forth on swing,
   As a skate's heel sweeps smooth on a bow-bend: the hurl
     and gliding
   Rebuffed the big wind. My heart in hiding
Stirred for a bird, – the achieve of, the mastery of the thing!

Brute beauty and valour and act, oh, air, pride, plume,
     here
   Buckle! AND the fire that breaks from thee then, a billion
Times told lovelier, more dangerous, O my chevalier!

   No wonder of it: shéer plód makes plough down sillion
Shine, and blue-bleak embers, ah my dear,
   Fall, gall themselves, and gash gold-vermilion.

'There's a certain Slant of light'

There's a certain Slant of light,
Winter Afternoons –
That oppresses, like the Heft
Of Cathedral Tunes –

Heavenly Hurt, it gives us –
We can find no scar,
But internal difference,
Where the Meanings, are –

None may teach it – Any –
'Tis the Seal Despair –
An imperial affliction
Sent us of the Air –

When it comes, the Landscape listens –
Shadows – hold their breath –
When it goes, 'tis like the Distance
On the look of Death –

Auguries of Innocence

To see a World in a Grain of Sand
And a Heaven in a Wild Flower,
Hold Infinity in the palm of your hand
And Eternity in a hour.
A Robin Red breast in a Cage
Puts all Heaven in a Rage.
A dove house fill'd with doves & Pigeons
Shudders Hell thro' all its regions.
A dog starv'd at his Master's Gate
Predicts the ruin of the State.
A Horse misus'd upon the Road
Calls to Heaven for Human blood.
Each outcry of the hunted Hare
A fibre from the Brain does tear.
A Skylark wounded in the wing,
A Cherubim does cease to sing.
The Game Cock clip'd & arm'd for fight
Does the Rising Sun affright.
Every Wolf's & Lion's howl
Raises from Hell a Human Soul.
The wild deer, wand'ring here & there,
Keeps the Human Soul from Care.
The Lamb misus'd breeds Public strife
And yet forgives the Butcher's Knife.
The Bat that flits at close of Eve
Has left the Brain that won't Believe.
The Owl that calls upon the Night
Speaks the Unbeliever's fright.
He who shall hurt the little Wren

Shall never be belov'd by Men.
He who the Ox to wrath has mov'd
Shall never be by Woman lov'd.
The wanton Boy that kills the Fly
Shall feel the Spider's enmity.
He who torments the Chafer's sprite
Weaves a Bower in endless Night.
The Catterpiller on the Leaf
Repeats to thee thy Mother's grief.
Kill not the Moth nor Butterfly,
For the Last Judgment draweth nigh.
He who shall train the Horse to War
Shall never pass the Polar Bar.
The Begger's Dog & Widow's Cat,
Feed them & thou wilt grow fat.
The Gnat that sings his Summer's song
Poison gets from Slander's tongue.
The poison of the Snake & Newt
Is the sweat of Envy's Foot.
The Poison of the Honey Bee
Is the Artist's Jealousy.
The Prince's Robes & Beggar's Rags
Are Toadstools on the Miser's Bags.
A truth that's told with bad intent
Beats all the Lies you can invent.
It is right it should be so;
Man was made for Joy & Woe;
And when this we rightly know
Thro' the World we safely go.
Joy & Woe are woven fine,
A Clothing for the Soul divine
Under every grief & pine
Runs a joy with silken twine.

The Babe is more than swadling Bands;
Throughout all these Human Lands
Tools were made, & Born were hands,
Every Farmer Understands.
Every Tear from Every Eye
Becomes a Babe in Eternity;
This is caught by Females bright
And return'd to its own delight.
The Bleat, the Bark, Bellow & Roar
Are Waves that Beat on Heaven's Shore.
The Babe that weeps the Rod beneath
Writes Revenge in realms of death.
The Beggar's Rags, fluttering in Air,
Does to Rags the Heavens tear.
The Soldier, arm'd with Sword & Gun,
Palsied strikes the Summer's Sun.
The poor Man's Farthing is worth more
Than all the Gold on Afric's Shore.
One Mite wrung from the Labrer's hands
Shall buy & sell the Miser's Lands:
Or, if protected from on high,
Does that whole Nation sell & buy.
He who mocks the Infant's Faith
Shall be mock'd in Age & Death.
He who shall teach the Child to Doubt
The rotting Grave shall ne'er get out.
He who respects the Infant's faith
Triumphs over Hell & Death.
The Child's Toys & the Old Man's Reasons
Are the Fruits of the Two seasons.
The Questioner, who sits so sly,
Shall never know how to reply.
He who replies to words of Doubt

Doth put the Light of Knowledge out.
The Strongest Poison ever known
Came from Caesar's Laurel Crown.
Nought can deform the Human Race
Like to the Armour's iron brace.
When Gold & Gems adorn the Plow
To peaceful Arts shall Envy Bow.
A Riddle or the Cricket's Cry
Is to Doubt a fit Reply.
The Emmet's Inch & Eagle's Mile
Make Lame Philosophy to smile.
He who Doubts from what he sees
Will ne'er Believe, do what you Please.
If the Sun & Moon should doubt,
They'd immediately Go out.
To be in a Passion you Good may do,
But no Good if a Passion is in you.
The Whore & Gambler, by the State
Licenc'd, build that Nation's Fate.
The Harlot's cry from Street to Street
Shall weave Old England's winding Sheet.
The Winner's Shout, the Loser's Curse,
Dance before dead England's Hearse.
Every Night & every Morn
Some to Misery are Born.
Every Morn & every Night
Some are Born to sweet delight.
Some are Born to sweet delight,
Some are Born to Endless Night.
We are led to Believe a Lie
When we see not Thro' the Eye
Which was Born in a Night to perish in a Night
When the Soul Slept in Beams of Light.

God Appears & God is Light
To those poor Souls who dwell in Night,
But does a Human Form Display
To those who Dwell in Realms of day.

W. E. HENLEY

Invictus

Out of the night that covers me,
   Black as the Pit from pole to pole,
I thank whatever gods may be
   For my unconquerable soul.

In the fell clutch of circumstance
   I have not winced nor cried aloud.
Under the bludgeonings of chance
   My head is bloody, but unbowed.

Beyond this place of wrath and tears
   Looms but the Horror of the shade,
And yet the menace of the years
   Finds, and shall find me, unafraid.

It matters not how strait the gate,
   How charged with punishments the scroll,
I am the master of my fate:
   I am the captain of my soul.

'The heavens themselves, the planets, and this centre'

The heavens themselves, the planets, and this centre
Observe degree, priority, and place,
Insisture, course, proportion, season, form,
Office, and custom, in all line of order:
And therefore is the glorious planet Sol
In noble eminence enthron'd and spher'd
Amidst the other; whose med'cinable eye
Corrects the ill aspects of planets evil,
And posts, like the commandment of a king,
Sans check, to good and bad: but when the planets
In evil mixture to disorder wander,
What plagues, and what portents, what mutiny,
What raging of the sea, shaking of earth,
Commotion in the winds, frights, changes, horrors,
Divert and crack, rend and deracinate
The unity and married calm of states
Quite from their fixture! O! when degree is shak'd.
Which is the ladder to all high designs,
The enterprise is sick. How could communities,
Degrees in schools, and brotherhoods in cities,
Peaceful commerce from dividable shores,
The primogenitive and due of birth,
Prerogative of age, crowns, sceptres, laurels,
But by degree, stand in authentic place?
Take but degree away, untune that string,
And, hark! what discord follows; each thing meets
In mere oppugnancy: the bounded waters
Should lift their bosoms higher than the shores,

And make a sop of all this solid globe:
Strength should be lord of imbecility,
And the rude son should strike his father dead:
Force should be right; or rather, right and wrong –
Between whose endless jar justice resides –
Should lose their names, and so should justice too.
Then every thing includes itself in power,
Power into will, will into appetite;
And appetite, a universal wolf,
So doubly seconded with will and power,
Must make perforce a universal prey,
And last eat up himself.

Strange Meeting

It seemed that out of battle I escaped
Down some profound dull tunnel, long since scooped
Through granites which titanic wars had groined.
Yet also there encumbered sleepers groaned,
Too fast in thought or death to be bestirred.
Then, as I probed them, one sprang up, and stared
With piteous recognition in fixed eyes,
Lifting distressful hands as if to bless.
And by his smile, I knew that sullen hall,
By his dead smile I knew we stood in Hell.
With a thousand pains that vision's face was grained;
Yet no blood reached there from the upper ground,
And no guns thumped, or down the flues made moan.
'Strange friend,' I said, 'here is no cause to mourn.'
'None,' said the other, 'save the undone years,
The hopelessness. Whatever hope is yours,
Was my life also; I went hunting wild
After the wildest beauty in the world,
Which lies not calm in eyes, or braided hair,
But mocks the steady running of the hour,
And if it grieves, grieves richlier than here.
For by my glee might many men have laughed,
And of my weeping something had been left,
Which must die now. I mean the truth untold,
The pity of war, the pity war distilled.
Now men will go content with what we spoiled.
Or, discontent, boil bloody, and be spilled.
They will be swift with swiftness of the tigress,
None will break ranks, though nations trek from progress.

Courage was mine, and I had mystery,
Wisdom was mine, and I had mastery;
To miss the march of this retreating world
Into vain citadels that are not walled
Then, when much blood had clogged their chariot-wheels
I would go up and wash them from sweet wells,
Even with truths that lie too deep for taint.
I would have poured my spirit without stint
But not through wounds; not on the cess of war.
Foreheads of men have bled where no wounds were.
I am the enemy you killed, my friend.
I knew you in this dark; for so you frowned
Yesterday through me as you jabbed and killed.
I parried; but my hands were loath and cold.
Let us sleep now . . . '

The Runaway

Once when the snow of the year was beginning to fall,
We stopped by a mountain pasture to say, 'Whose colt?'
A little Morgan had one forefoot on the wall,
The other curled at his breast. He dipped his head
And snorted at us. And then he had to bolt.
We heard the miniature thunder where he fled,
And we saw him, or thought we saw him, dim and gray,
Like a shadow against the curtain of falling flakes.
'I think the little fellow's afraid of the snow.
He isn't winter-broken. It isn't play
With the little fellow at all. He's running away.
I doubt if even his mother could tell him, "Sakes,
It's only weather." He'd think she didn't know!
Where is his mother? He can't be out alone.'
And now he comes again with clatter of stone,
And mounts the wall again with whited eyes
And all his tail that isn't hair up straight.
He shudders his coat as if to throw off flies.
'Whoever it is that leaves him out so late,
When other creatures have gone to stall and bin,
Ought to be told to come and take him in.'

Poem in October

It was my thirtieth year to heaven
Woke to my hearing from harbour and neighbour wood
  And the mussel pooled and the heron
      Priested shore
    The morning beckon
With water praying and call of seagull and rook
And the knock of sailing boats on the net webbed wall
    Myself to set foot
      That second
  In the still sleeping town and set forth.

  My birthday began with the water-
Birds and the birds of the winged trees flying my name
  Above the farms and the white horses
      And I rose
    In the rainy autumn
And walked abroad in a shower of all my days.
High tide and the heron dived when I took the road
    Over the border
      And the gates
  Of the town closed as the town awoke.

  A springful of larks in a rolling
Cloud and the roadside bushes brimming with whistling
  Blackbirds and the sun of October
      Summery
    On the hill's shoulder,
Here were fond climates and sweet singers suddenly
Come in the morning where I wandered and listened
    To the rain wringing

Wind blow cold
In the wood faraway under me.

Pale rain over the dwindling harbour
And over the sea wet church the size of a snail
With its horns through mist and the castle
Brown as owls
But all the gardens
Of spring and summer were blooming in the tall tales
Beyond the border and under the lark full cloud.
There could I marvel
My birthday
Away but the weather turned around.

It turned away from the blithe country
And down the other air and the blue altered sky
Streamed again a wonder of summer
With apples
Pears and red currants
And I saw in the turning so clearly a child's
Forgotten mornings when he walked with his mother
Through the parables
Of sun light
And the legends of the green chapels

And the twice told fields of infancy
That his tears burned my cheeks and his heart moved in
mine.
These were the woods the river and sea
Where a boy
In the listening
Summertime of the dead whispered the truth of his joy
To the trees and the stones and the fish in the tide.
And the mystery

        Sang alive
    Still in the water and singingbirds.

    And there could I marvel my birthday
Away but the weather turned around. And the true
    Joy of the long dead child sang burning
            In the sun.
        It was my thirtieth
Year to heaven stood there then in the summer noon
Though the town below lay leaved with October blood.
        O may my heart's truth
            Still be sung
    On this high hill in a year's turning.

The Small Bird to the Big

Fly up and away, large hawk,
To the eternal day of the abyss,
Belittling the night about the mountains.
Your eyes that are our terror
Are well employed about the secrets of the moon
Or the larger betrayals of the noon-day.
Do not stay just above
So that I must hide shuddering under inadequate twigs.
Sail through the dry smoke of volcanoes
Or the damp clouds if they will better encourage your
    feathers.
Then shall I weep with joy seeing your splendour,
Forget my cowardice, forget my weakness,
Feel the whole sunlight fall upon my tears.
I shall believe you a key to Paradise.
I shall believe you the chief light upon this dark grey world.

from the Japanese of C. Hatakeyama

Crossing the Water

Black lake, black boat, two black, cut-paper people.
Where do the black trees go that drink here?
Their shadows must cover Canada.

A little light is filtering from the water flowers.
Their leaves do not wish us to hurry:
They are round and flat and full of dark advice.

Cold worlds shake from the oar.
The spirit of blackness is in us, it is in the fishes.
A snag is lifting a valedictory, pale hand;

Stars open among the lilies.
Are you not blinded by such expressionless sirens?
This is the silence of astounded souls.

Musée des Beaux Arts

About suffering they were never wrong,
The Old Masters: how well they understood
Its human position; how it takes place
While someone else is eating or opening a window or
    just walking dully along;
How, when the aged are reverently, passionately
    waiting
For the miraculous birth, there always must be
Children who did not specially want it to happen,
    skating
On a pond at the edge of the wood:
They never forgot
That even the dreadful martyrdom must run its course
Anyhow in a corner, some untidy spot
Where the dogs go on with their doggy life and the
    torturer's horse
Scratches its innocent behind on a tree.

In Brueghel's *Icarus*, for instance: how everything turns
    away
Quite leisurely from the disaster; the ploughman may
Have heard the splash, the forsaken cry,
But for him it was not an important failure; the sun
    shone
As it had to on the white legs disappearing into the green
Water; and the expensive delicate ship that must have
    seen
Something amazing, a boy falling out of the sky,
Had somewhere to get to and sailed calmly on.

Not Waving but Drowning

Nobody heard him, the dead man,
But still he lay moaning:
I was much further out than you thought
And not waving but drowning.

Poor chap, he always loved larking
And now he's dead
It must have been too cold for him his heart gave way,
They said.

Oh, no no no, it was too cold always
(Still the dead one lay moaning)
I was much too far out all my life
And not waving but drowning.

'Seventy feet down'

Seventy feet down
The sea explodes upwards,
Relapsing, to slaver
Off landing-stage steps –
Running suds, rejoice!

Rocks writhe back to sight.
Mussels, limpets,
Husband their tenacity
In the freezing slither –
Creatures, I cherish you!

By day, sky builds
Grape-dark over the salt
Unsown stirring fields.
Radio rubs its legs,
Telling me of elsewhere:

Barometers falling,
Ports wind-shuttered,
Fleets pent like hounds,
Fires in humped inns
Kippering sea-pictures –

Keep it all off!
By night, snow swerves
(O loose moth world)
Through the stare travelling
Leather-black waters.

Guarded by brilliance
I set plate and spoon,
And after, divining-cards.
Lit shelved liners
Grope like mad worlds westward.

'Carry her over the water'

Carry her over the water,
   And set her down under the tree,
Where the culvers white all day and all night,
   And the winds from every quarter,
Sing agreeably, agreeably, agreeably of love.

Put a gold ring on her finger,
   And press her close to your heart,
While the fish in the lake their snapshots take,
   And the frog, that sanguine singer,
Sings agreeably, agreeably, agreeably of love.

The streets shall all flock to your marriage,
   The houses turn round to look,
The tables and chairs say suitable prayers,
   And the horses drawing your carriage
Sing agreeably, agreeably, agreeably of love.

Sandpiper

The roaring alongside he takes for granted,
and that every so often the world is bound to shake.
He runs, he runs to the south, finical, awkward,
in a state of controlled panic, a student of Blake.

The beach hisses like fat. On his left, a sheet
of interrupting water comes and goes
and glazes over his dark and brittle feet.
He runs, he runs straight through it, watching his toes.

– Watching, rather, the spaces of sand between them,
where (no detail too small) the Atlantic drains
rapidly backwards and downwards. As he runs,
he stares at the dragging grains.

The world is a mist. And then the world is
minute and vast and clear. The tide
is higher or lower. He couldn't tell you which.
His beak is focussed; he is preoccupied,

looking for something, something, something.
Poor bird, he is obsessed!
The millions of grains are black, white, tan, and gray,
mixed with quartz grains, rose and amethyst.

Dulce et Decorum Est

Bent double, like old beggars under sacks,
Knock-kneed, coughing like hags, we cursed through sludge,
Till on the haunting flares we turned our backs,
And towards our distant rest began to trudge.
Men marched asleep. Many had lost their boots,
But limped on, blood-shod. All went lame, all blind;
Drunk with fatigue; deaf even to the hoots
Of gas-shells dropping softly behind.

Gas! Gas! Quick boys! – An ecstasy of fumbling,
Fitting the clumsy helmets just in time,
But someone still was yelling out and stumbling
And floundering like a man in fire or lime. –
Dim through the misty panes and thick green light,
As under a green sea, I saw him drowning.
In all my dreams, before my helpless sight,
He plunges at me, guttering, choking, drowning.

If in some smothering dreams, you too could pace
Behind the wagon that we flung him in,
And watch the white eyes writhing in his face,
His hanging face, like a devil's sick of sin;
If you could hear, at every jolt, the blood
Come gargling from the froth-corrupted lungs,
Obscene as cancer, bitter as the cud
Of vile, incurable sores on innocent tongues, –
My friend, you would not tell with such high zest
To children ardent for some desperate glory,
The old Lie: *Dulce et decorum est*
Pro patria mori.

'Let me not to the marriage of true minds'

Let me not to the marriage of true minds
Admit impediments. Love is not love
Which alters when it alteration finds,
Or bends with the remover to remove:
O, no! it is an ever-fixed mark,
That looks on tempests and is never shaken;
It is the star to every wandering bark,
Whose worth's unknown, although his height be taken.
Love's not Time's fool, though rosy lips and cheeks
Within his bending sickle's compass come;
Love alters not with his brief hours and weeks,
But bears it out even to the edge of doom.
    If this be error, and upon me prov'd.
    I never writ, nor no man ever lov'd.

JOHN CROWE RANSOM

Bells for John Whiteside's Daughter

There was such speed in her little body,
And such lightness in her footfall,
It is no wonder her brown study
Astonishes us all.

Her wars were bruited in our high window.
We looked among orchard trees and beyond
Where she took arms against her shadow,
Or harried unto the pond

The lazy gees, like a snow cloud
Dripping their snow on the green grass,
Tricking and stopping, sleepy and proud,
Who cried in goose, Alas,

For the tireless heart within the little
Lady with rod that made them rise
From their noon apple-dreams and scuttle
Goose-fashion under the skies!

But now go the bells, and we are ready,
In one house we are sternly stopped
To say we are vexed at her brown study,
Lying so primly propped.

Journey of the Magi

'A cold coming we had of it,
Just the worst time of the year
For a journey, and such a long journey:
The ways deep and the weather sharp,
The very dead of winter.'
And the camels galled, sore-footed, refractory,
Lying down in the melting snow.
There were times we regretted
The summer palaces on slopes, the terraces,
And the silken girls bringing sherbet.
Then the camel men cursing and grumbling
And running away, and wanting their liquor and women,
And the night-fires going out, and the lack of shelters,
And the cities hostile and the towns unfriendly
And the villages dirty and charging high prices:
A hard time we had of it.
At the end we preferred to travel all night,
Sleeping in snatches,
With the voices singing in our ears, saying
That this was all folly.

Then at dawn we came down to a temperate valley,
Wet, below the snow line, smelling of vegetation,
With a running stream and a water-mill beating the
    darkness,
And three trees on the low sky.
And an old white horse galloped away in the meadow.
Then we came to a tavern with vine-leaves over the lintel,
Six hands at an open door dicing for pieces of silver,
And feet kicking the empty wine-skins.

But there was no information, so we continued
And arrived at evening, not a moment too soon
Finding the place; it was (you may say) satisfactory.

    All this was a long time ago, I remember,
And I would do it again, but set down
This set down
This: were we led all that way for
Birth or Death? There was a Birth, certainly,
We had evidence and no doubt. I had seen birth and death,
But had thought they were different; this Birth was
Hard and bitter agony for us, like Death, our death.
We returned to our places, these Kingdoms,
But no longer at ease here, in the old dispensation,
With an alien people clutching their gods.
I should be glad of another death.

Stopping by Woods
on a Snowy Evening

Whose woods these are I think I know.
His house is in the village, though;
He will not see me stopping here
To watch his woods fill up with snow.

My little horse must think it queer
To stop without a farmhouse near
Between the woods and frozen lake
The darkest evening of the year.

He gives his harness bells a shake
To ask if there is some mistake.
The only other sound's the sweep
Of easy wind and downy flake.

The woods are lovely, dark, and deep,
But I have promises to keep,
And miles to go before I sleep,
And miles to go before I sleep.

'Tir'd with all these, for restful death I cry'

Tir'd with all these, for restful death I cry
As to behold desert a beggar born.
And needy nothing trimm'd in jollity,
And purest faith unhappily forsworn.
And gilded honour shamefully misplac'd.
And maiden virtue rudely strumpeted.
And right perfection wrongfully disgraced.
And strength by limping sway disabled.
And art made tongue-tied by authority,
And folly – doctor-like – controlling skill,
And simple truth miscall'd simplicity,
And captive good attending captain ill:
    Tir'd with all these, from these would I be gone,
    Save that, to die, I leave my love alone.

Leda and the Swan

A sudden blow: the great wings beating still
Above the staggering girl, her thighs caressed
By the dark webs, her nape caught in his bill,
He holds her helpless breast upon his breast.

How can those terrified vague fingers push
The feathered glory from her loosening thighs?
And how can body, laid in that white rush,
But feel the strange heart beating where it lies?

A shudder in the loins engenders there
The broken wall, the burning roof and tower
And Agamemnon dead.
                 Being so caught up,
So mastered by the brute blood of the air,
Did she put on his knowledge with his power
Before the indifferent beak could let her drop?

EMILY DICKINSON

'This World is not Conclusion'

This World is not Conclusion.
A Species stands beyond –
Invisible, as Music –
But positive, as Sound –
It beckons, and it baffles –
Philosophy – don't know –
And through a Riddle, at the last –
Sagacity, must go –
To guess it, puzzles scholars –
To gain it, Men have borne
Contempt of Generations
And Crucifixion, shown –
Faith slips – and laughs, and rallies –
Blushes, if any see –
Plucks at a twig of Evidence –
And asks a Vane, the way –
Much Gesture, from the Pulpit –
Strong Hallelujahs roll –
Narcotics cannot still the Tooth
That nibbles at the soul –

Binsey Poplars

felled 1879

My aspens dear, whose airy cages quelled,
Quelled or quenched in leaves the leaping sun,
All felled, felled, are all felled;
    Of a fresh and following folded rank
        Not spared, not one
        That dandled a sandalled
        Shadow that swam or sank
On meadow and river and wind-wandering weed-
    winding bank.

O if we but knew what we do
        When we delve or hew –
    Hack and rack the growing green!
        Since country is so tender
    To touch, her being só slender,
    That, like this sleek and seeing ball
    But a prick will make no eye at all,

Where we, even where we mean
        To mend her we end her,
        When we hew or delve:
After-comers cannot guess the beauty been.
    Ten or twelve, only ten or twelve
        Strokes of havoc únselve
        The sweet especial scene,
      Rural scene, a rural scene,
      Sweet especial rural scene.

'Come let us mock at the great'

Come let us mock at the great
That had such burdens on the mind
And toiled so hard and late
To leave some monument behind,
Nor thought of the levelling wind.

Come let us mock at the wise;
With all those calendars whereon
They fixed old aching eyes,
They never saw how seasons run,
And now but gape at the sun.

Come let us mock at the good
That fancied goodness might be gay,
And sick of solitude
Might proclaim a holiday:
Wind shrieked – and where are they?

Mock mockers after that
That would not lift a hand maybe
To help good, wise or great
To bar that foul storm out, for we
Traffic in mockery.

The Simplon Pass

  – Brook and road
Were fellow-travellers in this gloomy Pass,
And with them did we journey several hours
At a slow step. The immeasurable height
Of woods decaying, never to be decayed,
The stationary blasts of waterfalls,
And in the narrow rent, at every turn,
Winds thwarting winds bewildered and forlorn,
The torrents shooting from the clear blue sky,
The rocks that muttered close upon our ears,
Black drizzling crags that spake by the wayside
As if a voice were in them, the sick sight
And giddy prospect of the raving stream,
The unfettered clouds and region of the heavens,
Tumult and peace, the darkness and the light –
Were all like workings of one mind, the features
Of the same face, blossoms upon one tree,
Characters of the great Apocalypse,
The types and symbols of Eternity,
Of first, and last, and midst, and without end.

The Darkling Thrush

I leant upon a coppice gate
　　When Frost was spectre-gray,
And Winter's dregs made desolate
　　The weakening eye of day.
The tangled bine-stems scored the sky
　　Like strings of broken lyres,
And all mankind that haunted nigh
　　Had sought their household fires.

The land's sharp features seemed to be
　　The Century's corpse outleant,
His crypt the cloudy canopy,
　　The wind his death-lament.
The ancient pulse of germ and birth
　　Was shrunken hard and dry,
And every spirit upon earth
　　Seemed fervourless as I.

At once a voice arose among
　　The bleak twigs overhead
In full-hearted evensong
　　Of joy illimited;
An aged thrush, frail, gaunt, and small,
　　In blast-beruffled plume,
Had chosen thus to fling his soul
　　Upon the growing gloom.

So little cause for carolings
　　Of such ecstatic sound
Was written on terrestrial things
　　Afar or nigh around,

That I could think there trembled through
   His happy good-night air
Some blessed Hope, whereof he knew
   And I was unaware.

'My love is as a fever, longing still'

My love is as a fever, longing still
For that which longer nurseth the disease;
Feeding on that which doth preserve the ill,
The uncertain sickly appetite to please.
My reason, the physician to my love,
Angry that his prescriptions are not kept,
Hath left me, and I desperate now approve
Desire is death, which physic did except.
Past cure I am, now Reason is past care.
And frantic-mad with evermore unrest;
My thoughts and my discourse as madmen's are,
At random from the truth vainly express'd;
   For I have sworn thee fair, and thought thee bright,
    Who art as black as hell, as dark as night.

Roger Casement

(after reading The Forged Casement Diaries *by Dr Maloney)*

I say that Roger Casement
Did what he had to do.
He died upon the gallows,
But that is nothing new.

Afraid they might be beaten
Before the bench of Time,
They turned a trick by forgery
And blackened his good name.

A perjurer stood ready
To prove their forgery true;
They gave it out to all the world,
And that is something new;

For Spring Rice had to whisper it,
Being their Ambassador,
And then the speakers got it
And writers by the score.

Come Tom and Dick, come all the troop
That cried it far and wide,
Come from the forger and his desk,
Desert the perjurer's side;

Come speak your bit in public
That some amends be made
To this most gallant gentleman
That is in quicklime laid.

'A slumber did my spirit seal'

A slumber did my spirit seal;
   I had no human fears:
She seemed a thing that could not feel
   The touch of earthly years.

No motion has she now, no force;
   She neither hears nor sees;
Rolled sound in earth's diurnal course,
   With rocks, and stones, and trees.

'Not mine own fears, nor the prophetic soul'

Not mine own fears, nor the prophetic soul
Of the wide world dreaming on things to come,
Can yet the lease of my true love control,
Suppos'd as forfeit to a confin's doom.
The mortal moon hath her eclipse endur'd,
And the sad augurs mock their own presage;
Incertainties now crown themselves assur'd,
And peace proclaims olives of endless age.
Now with the drops of this most balmy time
My love looks fresh, and Death to me subscribes,
Since, spite of him, I'll live in this poor rime,
While he insults o'er dull and speechless tribes:
    And thou in this shalt find thy monument,
      When tyrants' crests and tombs of brass are spent.

Song

Go, and catch a falling star,
  Get with child a mandrake root,
Tell me, where all past years are,
  Or who cleft the Devil's foot,
Teach me to hear mermaids singing,
  Or to keep off envy's stinging,
      And find
      What wind
Serves to advance an honest mind.

If thou be'est born to strange sights,
  Things invisible to see,
Ride ten thousand days and nights,
  Till age snow white hairs on thee,
Thou, when thou return'st, wilt tell me
All strange wonders that befell thee,
      And swear
      No where
Lives a woman true, and fair.

If thou find'st one, let me know,
  Such a pilgrimage were sweet,
Yet do not, I would not go,
  Though at next door we might meet,
Though she were true, when you met her,
And last, till you write your letter,
      Yet she
      Will be
False, ere I come, to two, or three.

EMILY DICKINSON

'A Wind that rose'

A Wind that rose
Though not a Leaf
In any Forest stirred
But with itself did cold engage
Beyond the Realm of Bird –
A Wind that woke a lone Delight
Like Separation's Swell
Restored in Arctic Confidence
To the Invisible –

To Autumn

Season of mists and mellow fruitfulness,
   Close bosom-friend of the maturing sun,
Conspiring with him how to load and bless
   With fruit the vines that round the thatch-eves run;
To bend with apples the mossed cottage-trees,
   And fill all fruit with ripeness to the core;
     To swell the gourd, and plump the hazel shells
   With a sweet kernel; to set budding more,
And still more, later flowers for the bees,
Until they think warm days will never cease,
     For Summer has o'er-brimmed their clammy cells.

Who hath not seen thee oft amid thy store?
   Sometimes whoever seeks abroad may find
Thee sitting careless on a granary floor,
   Thy hair soft-lifted by the winnowing wind;
Or on a half-reaped furrow sound asleep,
   Drowsed with the fume of poppies, while thy hook
     Spares the next swath and all its twinèd flowers;
And sometimes like a gleaner thou dost keep
   Steady thy laden head across a brook;
   Or by a cider-press, with patient look,
     Thou watchest the last oozings hours by hours.

Where are the songs of Spring? Ay, where are they?
   Think not of them, thou hast thy music too –
While barrèd clouds bloom the soft-dying day,
   And touch the stubble-plains with rosy hue:
Then in a wailful choir the small gnats mourn
   Among the river sallows, borne aloft

Or sinking as the light wind lives or dies;
And full-grown lambs loud bleat from hilly bourn;
Hedge-crickets sing; and now with treble soft
The red-breast whistles from a garden-croft;
And gathering swallows twitter in the skies.

WILLIAM BLAKE

The Sick Rose

O rose, thou art sick!
The invisible worm
That flies in the night,
In the howling storm,

Has found out thy bed
Of crimson joy:
And his dark secret love
Does thy life destroy.

Spring pools

These pools that, though in forests, still reflect
The total sky almost without defect,
And like the flowers beside them, chill and shiver,
Will like the flowers beside them soon be gone,
And yet not out by any brook or river,
But up by roots to bring dark foliage on.

The trees that have it in their pent-up buds
To darken nature and be summer woods –
Let them think twice before they use their powers
To blot out and drink up and sweep away
These flowery waters and these watery flowers
From snow that melted only yesterday.

'To be, or not to be: that is the question'

To be, or not to be: that is the question:
Whether 'tis nobler in the mind to suffer
The slings and arrows of outrageous fortune,
Or to take arms against a sea of troubles,
And by opposing end them? To die: to sleep;
No more; and, by a sleep to say we end
The heart-ache and the thousand natural shocks
That flesh is heir to, 'tis a consummation
Devoutly to be wish'd. To die, to sleep;
To sleep: perchance to dream: ay, there's the rub;
For in that sleep of death what dreams may come
When we have shuffled off this mortal coil,
Must give us pause. There's the respect
That makes calamity of so long life;
For who would bear the whips and scorns of time,
The oppressor's wrong, the proud man's contumely,
The pangs of dispriz'd love, the law's delay,
The insolence of office, and the spurns
The patient merit of the unworthy takes,
When he himself might his quietus make
With a bare bodkin? who would fardels bear,
To grunt and sweat under a weary life,
But that the dread of something after death,
The undiscover'd country from whose bourn
No traveller returns, puzzles the will,
And makes us rather bear those ills we have
Than fly to others that we know not of?
Thus conscience does make cowards of us all;
And thus the native hue of resolution

Is sicklied o'er with the pale cast of thought,
And enterprises of great pith and moment
With this regard their currents turn awry,
And lose the name of action.

Mr Apollinax

Ω τῆς καινότητος. Ἡράκλεις, τῆς παραδοξολογίας.
εὐμήχανος ἄνθρωπος.   *Lucian*

When Mr Apollinax visited the United States
His laughter tinkled among the teacups.
I thought of Fragilion, that shy figure among the
    birch-trees,
And of Priapus in the shrubbery
Gaping at the lady in the swing.
In the palace of Mrs Phlaccus, at Professor Channing-
    Cheetah's
He laughed like an irresponsible fœtus.
His laughter was submarine and profound
Like the old man of the sea's
Hidden under coral islands
Where worried bodies of drowned men drift down in the
    green silence,
Dropping from fingers of surf.

I looked for the head of Mr Apollinax rolling under a chair
Or grinning over a screen
With seaweed in its hair.
I heard the beat of centaur's hoofs over the hard turf
As his dry and passionate talk devoured the afternoon.
'He is a charming man' – 'But after all what did he mean?' –
'His pointed ears . . . He must be unbalanced.' –
'There was something he said that I might have
    challenged.'
Of dowager Mrs Phlaccus, and Professor and Mrs Cheetah
I remember a slice of lemon, and a bitten macaroon.

'To-morrow, and to-morrow, and to-morrow'

To-morrow, and to-morrow, and to-morrow,
Creeps in this petty pace from day to day,
To the last syllable of recorded time;
And all our yesterdays have lighted fools
The way to dusty death. Out, out, brief candle!
Life's but a walking shadow, a poor player
That struts and frets his hour upon the stage,
And then is heard no more; it is a tale
Told by an idiot, full of sound and fury,
Signifying nothing.

Death

Nor dread nor hope attend
A dying animal;
A man awaits his end
Dreading and hoping all;
Many times he died,
Many times rose again.
A great man in his pride
Confronting murderous men
Casts derision upon
Supersession of breath;
He knows death to the bone –
Man has created death.

Death by Water

Phlebas the Phoenician, a fortnight dead,
Forgot the cry of gulls, and the deep sea swell
And the profit and loss.
                              A current under sea
Picked his bones in whispers. As he rose and fell
He passed the stages of his age and youth
Entering the whirlpool.
                              Gentile or Jew
O you who turn the wheel and look to windward,
Consider Phlebas, who was once handsome and tall as you.

The Second Coming

Turning and turning in the widening gyre
The falcon cannot hear the falconer;
Things fall apart; the centre cannot hold;
Mere anarchy is loosed upon the world,
The blood-dimmed tide is loosed, and everywhere
The ceremony of innocence is drowned;
The best lack all conviction, while the worst
Are full of passionate intensity.

Surely some revelation is at hand;
Surely the Second Coming is at hand.
The Second Coming! Hardly are those words out
When a vast image out of *Spiritus Mundi*
Troubles my sight: somewhere in sands of the desert
A shape with lion body and the head of a man,
A gaze blank and pitiless as the sun,
Is moving its slow thighs, while all about it
Reel shadows of the indignant desert birds.
The darkness drops again; but now I know
That twenty centuries of stony sleep
Were vexed to nightmare by a rocking cradle,
And what rough beast, its hour come round at last,
Slouches towards Bethlehem to be born?

'There came a Wind like a Bugle'

There came a Wind like a Bugle –
It quivered through the Grass
And a Green Chill upon the Heat
So ominous did pass
We barred the Windows and the Doors
As from an Emerald Ghost –
The Doom's electric Moccasin
That very instant passed –
On a strange Mob of panting Trees
And Fences fled away
And Rivers where the Houses ran
Those looked that lived – that Day –
The Bell within the steeple wild
The flying tidings told –
How much can come
And much can go,
And yet abide the World!

'Our revels now are ended'

Our revels now are ended. These our actors,
As I foretold you, were all spirits and
Are melted into air, into thin air:
And, like the baseless fabric of this vision,
The cloud-capp'd towers, the gorgeous palaces,
The solemn temples, the great globe itself,
Yea, all which it inherit, shall dissolve
And, like this insubstantial pageant faded,
Leave not a rack behind. We are such stuff
As dreams are made on, and our little life
Is rounded with a sleep.

Neither Out Far nor In Deep

The people along the sand
All turn and look one way.
They turn their back on the land.
They look at the sea all day.

As long as it takes to pass
A ship keeps raising its hull;
The wetter ground like glass
Reflects a standing gull.

The land may vary more;
But wherever the truth may be –
The water comes ashore,
And the people look at the sea.

They cannot look out far.
They cannot look in deep.
But when was that ever a bar
To any watch they keep?

This Lunar Beauty

This lunar beauty
Has no history,
Is complete and early;
If beauty later
Bear any feature
It had a lover
And is another.

This like a dream
Keeps other time,
And daytime is
The loss of this;
For time is inches
And the heart's changes
Where ghost has haunted,
Lost and wanted.

But this was never
A ghost's endeavour
Nor, finished this,
Was ghost at ease;
And till it pass
Love shall not near
The sweetness here
Nor sorrow take
His endless look.

A Musical Instrument

What was he doing, the great god Pan,
   Down in the reeds by the river?
Spreading ruin and scattering ban,
Splashing and paddling with hoofs of a goat,
And breaking the golden lilies afloat
   With the dragon-fly on the river.

He tore out a reed, the great god Pan,
   From the deep cool bed of the river:
The limpid water turbidly ran,
And the broken lilies a-dying lay,
And the dragon-fly had fled away,
   Ere he brought it out of the river.

High on the shore sate the great god Pan,
   While turbidly flowed the river;
And hacked and hewed as a great god can,
With his hard bleak steel at the patient reed,
Till there was not a sign of a leaf indeed
   To prove it fresh from the river.

He cut it short, did the great god Pan.
   (How tall it stood in the river!)
Then drew the pith, like the heart of a man,
Steadily from the outside ring,
And notched the poor dry empty thing
   In holes, as he sate by the river.

'This is the way,' laughed the great god Pan.
   (Laughed while he sate by the river,)
'The only way, since gods began

To make sweet music, they could succeed.'
Then, dropping his mouth to a hole in the reed,
    He blew in power by the river.

Sweet, sweet, sweet, O Pan!
    Piercing sweet by the river!
Blinding sweet, O great god Pan!
The sun on the hill forgot to die,
And the lilies revived, and the dragon-fly
    Came back to dream on the river.

Yet half a beast is the great god Pan,
    To laugh as he sits by the river,
Making a poet out of a man;
The true gods sigh for the cost and pain –
For the reed which grows nevermore again
    As a reed with the reeds in the river.

Acknowledgements

W. H. AUDEN: for 'Carry her over the water', 'Musée des Beaux Arts, 'Stop all the clocks', 'The Fall of Rome' and 'This Lunar Beauty' from *Collected Poems*, to Faber and Faber Ltd. JOHN BETJEMAN: for 'A Subaltern's Love Song' and 'Meditation on the A30' from *Collected Poems*, to John Murray (Publishers) Ltd. ELIZABETH BISHOP: for 'Sandpiper', to Farrar, Straus & Giroux. WALTER DE LA MARE: for 'An Epitaph', to the Literary Trustees and The Society of Authors. KEITH DOUGLAS: for 'How to Kill', to Oxford University Press. T. S. ELIOT: for 'Death by Water' (from *The Waste Land*), 'Journey of the Magi', 'La Figlia Che Piange', 'Lines for an Old Man', 'Marina' and 'Mr Apollinax' from *Collected Poems 1909–1962*, to Mrs Valerie Eliot and Faber and Faber Ltd. WILLIAM EMPSON: for 'The Small Bird to the Big', to Chatto & Windus and Random House UK Ltd. ROBERT FROST: for 'Neither Far Out Nor In Deep', 'Provide, Provide', 'Spring Pools', 'Stopping by Woods', 'The Road Not Taken' and 'The Runaway', to Jonathan Cape Ltd. and Random House UK Ltd. THOMAS HARDY: for 'Beeny Cliff' and 'The Darkling Thrush', to Macmillan Publishers Ltd. SEAMUS HEANEY: for 'The Skunk' from *Field Work*, to Faber and Faber Ltd. F. R. HIGGINS: for 'Song for The Clatter Bones', to Mrs Mary Higgins. A. E. HOUSMAN: for excerpt from *A Shropshire Lad*, to The Society of Authors. RUDYARD KIPLING: for 'James I' and 'The Way through the Woods', to A. P. Watt on behalf of the National Trust. D. H. LAWRENCE: for 'Piano', to Laurence Pollinger Ltd and the Estate of Frieda Lawrence Ravagli. SYLVIA PLATH: for 'Crossing the Water', to Faber and Faber Ltd. EZRA POUND: for 'The Return' from *Collected Shorter Poems*, to Faber and Faber Ltd. JOHN CROWE RANSOM: for 'Bells for John Whiteside's Daughter' and 'Blue Girls' from *Selected Poems*, to Carcanet Press. STEVIE SMITH: for 'Not Waving but Drowning' from *The Collected Poems of Stevie Smith* (Penguin 20th-century Classics), to James MacGibbon. DYLAN THOMAS: for 'A Refusal to Mourn the Death by Fire of a Child in London' and 'Poem in October' from *Collected Poems*, to The Trustees of the Copyrights of Dylan Thomas and The Orion Publishing Group. R. S. THOMAS: for

'Here', to J. M. Dent and Sons Ltd. W. B. YEATS: for 'A woman's beauty is like a white', 'Come let us mock at the great', 'Death', 'Easter 1916', 'He Hears the Cry of the Sedge', 'Leda and the Swan', 'Roger Casement' and 'The Second Coming', to A. P. Watt on behalf of Michael Yeats. ANDREW YOUNG: for 'Field Glasses' from *The Poetical Works of Andrew Young*, ed. Lowbury and Young (Secker & Warburg, 1985), to The Andrew Young Estate.

Index of Poets

Index of First Lines